W9-BJN-124

The Computer Age

Books by the Editors of FORTUNE

USA—The Permanent Revolution (1951)
Is Anybody Listening? (1952)
Why Do People Buy? (1953)
A Guide to Modern Management Methods (1954)
The Changing American Market (1954)
The Mighty Force of Research (1956)
The Fabulous Future (1956)
The Executive Life (1956)
The Art of Success (1956)
Adventures in Small Business (1957)
The Amazing Advertising Business (1957)
The Exploding Metropolis (1958)
The New World of Math (1959)
Markets of the Sixties (1960)
Great American Scientists (1961)
The Space Industry (1962)
The Insiders: A Stockholder's Guide to Wall Street (1962)
Fortune's Guide to Personal Investing (1963)
Corporations in Crisis (1963)

The Computer Age

And Its Potential for Management

GILBERT BURCK
and the Editors of FORTUNE

HARPER & ROW, *Publishers*
NEW YORK, EVANSTON, AND LONDON

Diagrams by Max Gschwind

LIBRARY OF CONGRESS CATALOG CARD NUMBER: 64-25148

Contents

Charts

Preface

WORK ON THIS BOOK began in the autumn of 1963. Although we at *Fortune*, over several years, had faithfully chronicled the growing role of the electronic digital computer in the so-called information revolution, the machine suddenly loomed up into a colossal scientific, industrial, and social phenomenon. As the twentieth anniversary of its invention approached, we decided the time had come to stand back and take a new and appraising look at this great invention, first in a series of magazine pieces and finally in the present book.

I volunteered for the job, but not because I knew any more about computers than the average journalist. The editors of *Fortune* have always believed that an informed writer whose enthusiasm has not been dulled by excessive familiarity can bring a glow of discovery or a new perspective to a subject without being naïve about it; and that provided he works hard enough to get under the skin of his facts, he can even achieve the accuracy and sophistication of the technical specialist. Educating a writer to behave this way is onerous and expensive, but at least he is a writer, which the technical expert all too often is not. As the world's stock of specialized knowledge increases, the man of highly specialized knowledge seems to find it harder and harder to communicate effectively.

After a preliminary immersion in the subject of computers, including a 70-hour week in I.B.M.'s Executive Concept course at Poughkeepsie, New York, I convinced myself and my colleagues that the computer had got far beyond the understanding of even the very well-informed layman. My job as a professional communicator seemed obvious. At the risk of telling several hundred or more computer specialists what they already knew, my task was to begin by appraising the role of the machine for the well-informed layman as thoroughly as I could, first in a single magazine article. We sought and received the help of John Pfeiffer, author of *The Thinking Machine* and a man who has written a great deal about the computer without writing like a technical specialist; his article is the third chapter of this book. Thus, the book was not turned out as an ordinary one, with all or most of the research material in hand before the first chapter was begun. The attentive reader will consequently note a few overlaps or repetitions. The subject being what it is, they may be useful and welcome.

As is more or less usual, the first drafts were copiously revised simply because many people suggested convincingly that revision would improve them. There were my editors, Louis Banks and Duncan Norton-Taylor, who spotted defects that even a highly self-critical writer can detect only after he has allowed his hot copy to cool off for a few days. There was Lorraine Carson, my research assistant, who handled my nascent extravagances in such a way that I was generally under the impression I had discovered my own mistakes.

Above all, there were more than a hundred authorities and professionals in universities, corporations, consultants' offices and computer companies, most of whom we interviewed at length. Many are mentioned, quoted, or discussed in this book; they received first drafts of the pieces, along with explicit invitations to work their will on them. They handed us compliments, but what is more important they also handed us a lot of invaluable comments and criticisms; for such we are enormously grateful. These comments and criticisms, it should be added, were easier to accept than to incorporate into the writing. It takes a lot of sweating to add a new or contradictory idea to a passage that has been constructed carefully for its total effect, particularly one that has been illuminated by a just analogy or relevant figure of speech. Like altering an old house, the process takes more time than building a new one; but it is well worth the agony.

At such times the conscientious nonfiction writer finds himself envying the fiction writer, who can summarily choose the facts that suit his purpose and disregard those that do not. For unlike the facts of fiction, the so-called hard facts of real life are not really hard at all. They are elusive and transient, and their shape and import change with every circumstance; but it is this coyness that makes them so provocative. That I guess is why, to paraphrase Sam Johnson, he who is tired of the facts of life is tired of life itself.

G.B.

New York City
September 1964

The Computer Age

1

The Boundless Age of the Computer

"THE ELECTRONIC COMPUTER," says Ray Eppert, president of Burroughs Corporation, "has a more beneficial potential for the human race than any other invention in history." This colossal judgment might seem merely the occupational extravagance of an ardent computer salesman, which Ray Eppert is. But the Burroughs chief weighed his words with care, and put the case for the computer no more extravagantly than many a Ph.D. with reservations in his mind and footnotes in his voice. More and more people with special competence in computer circles are coming to the same conclusion.

What, the computer more beneficial than the printing press or the wheel? More than the steam engine or the dynamo and electric motor, to say nothing of atomic power? An impressive case can be made for putting the computer at the top of the list—given the qualification that the latest great technical innovation often exerts the greatest impact because it feeds on previous achievements. The dynamo obviously never would have amounted to so much if a steam prime mover had not existed. The computer itself is classified as a product of the electrical manufacturing industry, and without that industry's tremendous advances it would have remained a challenging but impractical museum piece. A hundred and thirty years ago the functions of the modern computer were understood by a few British pioneers, but it remained for the vacuum tube to make the computer practicable, and for diodes and transistors to make it the prodigy it is today.

Certainly no other single item of capital goods has changed the basic terms of so many human activities in so short a time. Within a few years, as the engine of modern information technology, it has profoundly altered the techniques of science, has begun to make government efficient, and has provided a new basis for the strategies of national defense. Above all, it is radically changing business' production methods and the art and science of management. Although the machine is the bête noire of critics who fear it will accelerate unemployment and compound the worst problems of modern society, it seems destined to shine as a powerful instrument for making business more creative and efficient and hence for raising the nation's real income per person, for eliminating a vast amount of drudgery, and for increasing leisure. In short, for measurably expanding free man's range of choices, which by definition is the goal of any good society.

One characteristic of the computer that makes it unique

among technical achievements is that it has forced men to think about what they are doing with clarity and precision. A man cannot instruct the computer to perform usefully until he has arduously thought through what he is up to in the first place, and where he wants to go from there. Even scientists, once they have wrestled with a computer's demands on knowledge and logic, are astonished to discover how much of their mental activity travels in ruts. The rethinking process gets more difficult as the computer gets better. Wherever the machine is used, it is improving enormously the quantity and quality of human cogitation; and it is rapidly becoming a kind of Universal Disciplinarian.

THE GREAT PROCESSOR

A convenient way to explain the machine is to compare it with man himself. In his long and unfinished struggle to master his physical environment, man progressed by processing knowledge. That is to say, instead of relying wholly on his favorite haruspex or gut reader, he learned to gather and differentiate knowledge, and so to transform it into something useful. It is hardly more than a tautology to observe that practically all the wrong decisions over the centuries, from Darius' attack at Marathon to the birth of the Edsel, have been at bottom the result of insufficient or inadequately processed knowledge. On the other hand, the gods themselves have been on the side of mortals who knew enough not to bother them with everything—who could process knowledge well enough to relate cause and effect and count consequences with tolerable accuracy. Given adequate knowledge, man learned to rely more and more on deductive or analytical judgment, which proceeds from a body of facts, and less and less on guesses and intuitive judgment, which he necessarily uses when a lot of relevant facts are missing.

The electronic computer is basically a device for ingesting, judging, and otherwise processing or usefully modifying knowledge. Thus it enlarges brainpower even as other man-made machines enlarge muscle power. Like man, the computer expresses knowledge in terms of symbols; man's symbols are letters and numbers, and the machine's symbols are electromagnetic impulses that represent letters and numbers.* Although man must usually instruct or program the machine minutely, its chief present advantage is that it can manipulate symbols a million times faster than a man with pencil and paper, and can make calculations in a few minutes that might take man alone a century. Richard Hamming of Bell Telephone Laboratories has remarked that the difference between doing a calculation by hand and by computer is the difference between having one dollar and having a million. Sometimes the difference is infinite; only a computer can calculate swiftly enough to analyze the data from a satellite, or to enable man to control the flight of a missile.

But the computer adds more than lightning calculation and fact sorting to man's brainpower. Besides an arithmetic unit, it is equipped with a memory that holds its knowledge on call, a stored program device that follows a set of instructions by code, and control units through which it reads and executes instructions. Its most portentous faculty is what

* There are two categories of computers: (1) the analog, which measures and compares quantities in one operation and has no memory; and (2) the digital, which solves problems by counting precisely and sequentially and has a memory. The electric analog computer is about fifty years old, enjoys a big and growing use in simulation and process control, and is "hybridized" with digital computers in some applications. But it accounts for a very small percentage of the market and its potentialities at present are not so catholic as those of the digital machine. Unless this book specifies otherwise, it means digital when it says computer.

is called the conditional transfer, or sometimes the branch or jump operation, which allows it to choose from alternatives. Without the transfer, the machine must run brutelike through all the alternatives in a given problem to hit the right one; with the transfer, it can *assess* and then *conclude*. In effect, the machine searches its memory and makes judgments and in general acts remarkably like a sentient being. That is how the computer can make selective payroll deductions, and beat the house at blackjack, and why it is indispensable in cybernation, or the process of automatic communication and control.

Most problems presented to computers are algorithmic or "well structured"—that is, problems leading inevitably to a conclusion, such as making out bills, calculating trajectories, or solving equations. But now computer men are trying to make the machine do more. It is true that the computer can perform only what we know how to order it to perform. But since it embodies a conditional transfer, suppose we instruct it to learn from experience. Professor Herbert A. Simon of Carnegie Institute of Technology, among others, has in effect done just that. He has demonstrated to the satisfaction of a lot of people that he can instruct a computer to solve relatively "ill-structured" problems, which are the kind that infest all life, by using rules of thumb and by trial-and-error search. In the new jargon of the computer world, Simon has made the machine behave "heuristically" ("serving to discover") as well as algorithmically.

Thus Simon and the other dedicated computer men are writing of machines "which do not merely substitute brute force for human cunning. Increasingly they imitate—and in some cases improve upon—human cunning." Some talk of the immortal brain, or a computer whose external memory store can be expanded indefinitely, to include the wisdom of the ages. This computer would be a paragon of intelligence, able to relate all its stored knowledge accurately, to reason without being corrupted by emotion, to discover new relationships between old things, to solve more of the world's problems than anyone solved before, even to create works of art. Man would be superior to this machine god, the joke goes, only because he presumably could still pull the plug or throw the switch.

Such extrapolations, so uncomfortably reminiscent of the androids of science fiction, have aroused a storm of opposition, and revived in intellectual circles hoary textbook issues like free will vs. determinism and vitalism vs. mechanism. At one extreme are people like the late Norbert Wiener, a pioneer in computers, who popularized the word cybernetics but later solemnly warned that computers can be improved to the point where they will get out of man's control. At the other extreme are embattled skeptics who denounce the notion that machines can ever really simulate human thinking. In between is a group taking various potshots at the computer's abuses, real and imaginary, including the "dire threat" it presents to employment and the social order.

A GAME FOR MENTAL GEAR SHIFTERS

The "acceptance" of the electronic computer, appropriately enough, has been extraordinary if not unique. Unlike some other great innovations, which have needed anywhere from fifty to one hundred years to assume their role in the scheme of things, it has taken a very big role in a few years, and is headed for a vastly bigger one. A dozen years ago there were fewer than two score machines in the land; today there are about 16,000 installations; including accessory devices, they are probably worth around $7 billion. Most other great inventions have flourished mainly within single industries; this ecumenically versatile one is already indispensable in most important human activities. Several thousand distinct applications have been catalogued, and the list is out of date before it leaves the presses. Never before has a single device generated in so short a time so many technical papers, pamphlets, articles, and books; merely to scan the daily flow of new and important information about the computer, to say nothing of the bales of quasi-information about it, is beyond the capacity of anything but the computer itself. Yet only a small minority of technical experts wholly understand the machine; the vast majority of enlightened laymen know it mainly as a kind of mysterious twelve-foot refrigerator with blinking lights and whirring tapes. The gulf of incomprehension between the experts and laymen is doubtless far greater than the gulf between Christopher Columbus and the savage Indians who knelt to worship him on San Salvador.

Never before, probably, has a single innovation generated such a technically sophisticated, talented, competitive, expansion-minded, and well-heeled manufacturing business. Staffed by thousands of men with advanced degrees, confidently risking billions on research and development, jubilantly peddling machines that embody "sensational" advances and yet are almost obsolete by the time they hit the market, the computer industry is a union of science and business that makes the auto and appliance industries in their great old days seem like a bunch of kids playing mumblety-peg. The game today is surely one for men who know how to shift mental gears swiftly. If anything is changing faster than computerized business, it is the business of making computers. About 60 cents of every dollar spent on computer hardware now goes for the central processor, and the rest for "peripheral" equipment like input-output devices, files, and communications. But in a decade, according to the Diebold Group, management advisers, peripheral equipment will account for 75 or 80 cents of the hardware dollar. At the same time, the "software" or programming business seems to be growing even faster than the hardware industry; some predict that software volume will soon surpass hardware volume.

The industry is dominated and in a way protected by International Business Machines, which a dozen years ago in a remarkably skillful shift changed itself from the world's biggest punched-card office-machine company into the biggest electronic-computer company. I.B.M.'s competitors, which include such names as Sperry Rand's Univac Division, R.C.A., G.E., Burroughs, Minneapolis-Honeywell, N.C.R., and Control Data, are heavily armed with brains, ambition, and money. Their so-called assault on fortress I.B.M., which will be the subject of a later chapter, is gathering way as one of the most arresting struggles in business history.

TO BUSINESS, ON A PLATTER

The benefits that the computer has conferred on government and science are tolerably familiar, and may be covered briefly. For government the machine has done something that nothing else has ever done before, at least on a big scale: it has vastly improved the productivity of bureaucracy. In 1951, for instance, the Census Bureau bought a Univac I. By 1960, fortified with several more, the bureau needed only half as many people to do twice the work that 4,500 had done in 1950. The federal government, including the Defense Department and the AEC, now uses some 1,250 electronic computers, against 730 as recently as 1961, and expects to be using 1,500 or more within two years. The computer's contribution to government efficiency does not get into the national productivity figures, however, because statistics still assume that government output per man-hour remains constant.

To science and technology the electronic computer has been a colossal and unprecedented boon. Chemistry, weather forecasts, physics, education, missile design and operation—these are only a few fields in which the machine is responsible for totally new techniques and achievements. Before Bell Laboratories' scientists possessed computers, they spent months building laboratory pilot plants of transmission systems; now they simulate systems by constructing models on paper and running the figures through a computer, and they come up with the ideal system in a matter of days. About 10 per cent of the laboratories' experiments are performed on the computer, but in time, Richard Hamming estimates, perhaps 90 per cent of them will be.

The combination of World War II and the computer put the military into business in more ways than one. War itself, these days, is only a highly unfriendly kind of business. Of the 800 or more computers operated by the Defense Department, the Air Force employs more than 400. The largest group of these—about 125—manages the Air Force's worldwide inventory, which is worth no less than $12 billion. Computers helped the Air Force Logistics Command to reduce its head count to 146,000 from 212,000 in 1956; and one of the most advanced inventory controls anywhere is its Automatic Resupply Logistic System, which balances inventories by automatically sending out shipping notices whenever the stock of an item anywhere descends to a given level.

Clemenceau, who remarked that war is too important to

be left to the generals, would be agreeably amazed by the Air Force's SAGE (Semi-Automatic Ground Environment), set up in 1957 to protect the U.S. from a surprise air attack. Using strategically located computers to interpret information gathered by radar, SAGE automatically identifies and categorizes as friend or foe every craft in the air above the United States and Canada, supplies details of its speed, specifications, location, and physical environment. If necessary, it alerts Air Force planes, assigns targets, or dispatches intercepting missiles. Thus SAGE simulates a large business system with strategically located division offices, all bound together by an information-and-control network. This network, in effect, not only keeps the home office aware of regional and system fluctuations in sales, costs, inventories, and profits, but takes the necessary steps to correct imbalances.

MACHINES NEED MANAGERS

Such military demonstrations of computer ability, together with the research and development done to produce scientific and military systems, have enormously accelerated the business world's "acceptance" of the computer. In 1954, when experts were estimating optimistically that as many as fifty companies would eventually use computers, General Electric's new Louisville appliance plant took delivery on the first data processor used by a private company, a Sperry Rand Univac. Today the vast bulk of American computers operate in the plants and offices of several thousand companies. In both 1963 and 1964, U.S. business absorbed more than 1,000 systems, worth about $1.7 billion including peripheral equipment; and the accompanying software cost more than $1.2 billion. Although a few industry specialists think that business installations will remain on a plateau for a few years while these companies absorb what they have, others see a steadily rising volume. In any event, all predict that delivered value of business computers will rise sharply in a few years, and even double or triple by the early 1970s.

By no means have all installations to date been unqualified blessings. In a fairly recent study of more than 300 installations in 27 major manufacturing companies, McKinsey & Company, the management consultants, found that 18 of the companies were not earning enough on the computers to cover their investment, and apparently U.S. business as a whole was making little if anything on them. Overselling was not the main problem, though doubtless there was some. The principal reason for the trouble seems to have been that management, particularly top management, did not give enough study and thought to the potential of computers.

The success stories help explain the failures, and why there are steadily fewer failures. Almost invariably the companies that made the machines pay off put computer operation decisions in the hands of senior managers. These men did not look on the machine as a gift package that needed only to be plugged in, but subjected themselves to its rigorous discipline. They analyzed their businesses and kept looking for new ways to use the computer even when they were employing the machines profitably on routine jobs. They were also willing to reorient their operating routines and their company organizations, if necessary, to exploit the computer. They represent the kind of manager, many are convinced, who will be running U.S. business tomorrow. "The time when executives could fool around with the machine is gone," says one computer-company officer. "Either they make the computer an indispensable part of their business, or they become a dispensable part of business."

This somewhat dogmatic conclusion on the whole seems justified. The machine is developing many more capabilities than anyone dreamed of a few years ago, and no business organization can afford to bypass them summarily. The indefatigably resourceful manufacturers are developing new "peripheral" equipment, making more tractable machines, finding countless new uses for them, introducing models with startling new powers, and reducing unit costs of using them. And many large users of the machines have taken the initiative and developed applications so original that they regard them as proprietary, and refuse to talk about them.

Most of the profitable operations are still confined to such "routine" jobs as fulfilling payrolls, making out accounts payable and receivable, and processing insurance data, but even these applications are growing vastly more refined. Thousands of insurance policyholders pay their premiums annually, semi-annually, quarterly, monthly; some die, some marry. When billing them, an insurance company's machine has to update information about them. Until recently the data was punched into cards, and the machine had to shuffle through the cards seriatim until it found the right ones. Now random-access storage devices enable the machine to snatch policy records and extract the information it needs in the twinkling of an eye.

LIFE WITH THE FEEDBACK PRINCIPLE

Much more portentous, however, are several sophisticated developments still in their infancy but which promise to change business methods radically. One is the information feedback principle, which some regard as one of the world's most important concepts because it governs everything done by individuals, groups, and machines in the process of adjusting to one another. A simple mechanical example of the principle at work is the common thermostat, where temperature and furnace continually interact to keep heat at a predetermined level. A more complex example is a computer-controlled oil refinery. Hundreds of measuring devices lead to the machine, which, having been given thousands of instructions on how to react to the readings of the measuring devices, instantaneously applies heat or pressure or otherwise adjusts the controls. Because it keeps on reacting and making adjustments instantaneously, it never has to make large adjustments.

Owing in part to the efforts of Professor Jay Forrester of M.I.T., the feedback principle is also being combined with the computer to create an important management tool, chiefly by eliminating delays in communication. Take inventories, which pose a prime problem for both corporations and the economy. To show how difficult it ordinarily is to keep stocks in line with demand, computer people like to play an inventory game. In its simple form, several people participate. One represents a retailer, two represent distributors, and a fourth the factory warehouse manager. Others represent customers and the factory. When goods are bought by the customers, a chain of events begins that ends in the factory the equivalent of five weeks later. The game quickly fouls up. Owing to the long lead time, retailers, distributors, and warehouse managers misjudge their needs because they do not know what happens until some time after it has happened. They find themselves with either insufficient or excessive inventories. Thus a tiny disturbance at the sales end results in a big dislocation at the factory. In real life the inevitable adjustment proves very expensive. Ill-adjusted inventories, for individual companies, result in high costs or worse; for the economy as a whole, excessive inventories usually result in recession, which in its majestic impartiality hits companies that have managed to keep their inventories in line—though not nearly so hard as those that have not.

The use of computers in inventory management already seems to have had a stabilizing effect on the economy. The national ratio of inventory to sales has not changed much over the years, but many businesses, notably auto dealers, must carry larger stocks to afford wider ranges of choice; in other words, better inventory control has enabled manufacturers to offer better service without increasing costs and risks. Although relatively few companies are yet using advanced inventory systems, nearly all are big companies, and their restraint in inventory buildup is doubtless one of the strong supports of the economy's current salubrity. What might happen when most companies use computers to control inventories is an exhilarating speculation.

Another portentous development is simulation. Note that the inventory game, by simulating a real inventory system, allows the players to study its faults and correct them with computers. In much the same way, simulation is being applied to management problems. Professor Forrester, using one minute of computer time, has simulated the operation of an entire business over a period of 400 weeks. In real life, a description of a company's operations is fed into the computer, which produces several alternatives for decisions about financial, manpower, product-flow, and other problems. From these alternatives, management merely has to choose the best ones. Some oil companies eliminate most if not all of the guesswork in planning new service stations by simulating two or three years of operation at proposed sites, and then picking the sites that promise to pay off the best.

Ken Powell, I.B.M.'s manager of educational research,

says that every application of a computer is a simulation; properly understood, it provides unique insights into business. Companies are catching on. What often happens, says Powell, is that a businessman starts with a payroll job whose purpose is merely to get the checks to his employees. He begins to see how the computer can be used to analyze distribution and manufacturing, and then how it can do routine inventory work. Next it dawns on him that in programming the computer to do certain jobs, he must in effect set up models of parts of his business. In the end he finds himself making experimental models of his company's activities. From these he can make decisions about them that he could have made no other way; instead of relying on guesses and intuition, he now can go ahead on logical deductions from facts.

Finally, there are such new methods of scheduling work as Program Evaluation and Review Technique (PERT) and the Critical Path Method (CPM), which enable managers to control immediately and in detail the timing and budgets of complex and dispersed construction projects involving as many as 30,000 different steps. PERT is given credit for accelerating the development of the Polaris missile by two years, and CPM is being widely used in the construction industry. Without the computer's ability to calculate and assess at superhuman speeds, these time- and money-saving systems would be impossible.

Such are some of the commercial avenues down which computers are leading. As yet, these avenues have not joined in the construction of the "total" system about which some computer men descanted so persuasively a few years ago. A total system, as the name suggests, would be one in which all a company's inputs and outputs are automatically coordinated. Orders would result in the appropriate allocations of labor and materials, and inventories would be appropriately adjusted. Payments and bills would be mailed. Markets would be gauged, and managers would have only to read the tape and make key decisions. Perhaps the nearest thing to a total system is SAGE; but business is much more complex than cold war, and it will be a long while before the business equivalent of SAGE is working. Meantime, there is plenty to be done in making use of existing techniques and systems.

THE "GENERAL PROBLEM SOLVER"

Since the machine can guide and fortify and even make some decisions, what will it do to the men who now make the decisions? The computerized executive world twenty years from now is a special interest of Herbert Simon, who was a social scientist specializing in administrative behavior when the computer was a cloud on the horizon. Simon takes the viewpoint that executive decision making is analogous to the behavior of the computer. He therefore divides it into (1) solving programmed or well-structured problems, and (2) solving non-specifically programmed or ill-structured problems. Examples of the former: clerical and other routine jobs, such as ordering office supplies, pricing orders by catalogue, and working out payroll deductions—plus a long list of somewhat less repetitive jobs, such as balancing assembly lines, determining the product mix for an oil refinery, planning manufacturing and employment schedules, and even choosing trust portfolio investments. Examples of ill-structured problems: consequential decisions for which there is no exact precedent, such as a general's decision to attack, or a company manager's to mount a sales campaign.

Mathematical techniques and the electronic computer are radically changing routine programmed decision making.

Now they are pushing into many middle-management decision areas, such as those in manufacturing and warehousing. Before long, Simon says, they will make most of a company's programmed decisions, just as they will control manufacturing operations. But as big a revolution, he predicts, will occur when heuristic techniques enable the computer to make more non-specifically programmed decisions, which are the kind on which the experienced manager exercises his judgment and intuition. A good example of decision making or problem solving on the heuristic borderline is the prevailing practice of assigning computers instead of engineers to modify the designs of standard electric motors according to the customers' specifications. When the order comes in, the computer searches through its memory, finds the right design, and modifies the design to fit the need.

In more complex decision making, such as deciding on company strategy, ill-structured problems must be broken down into goals or subgoals, and means must be related to ends. Simon, together with his associates Allen Newell and J. C. Shaw, in projects sponsored by Rand Corporation and Carnegie Tech, has done a lot of work in analyzing complex problem solving and in instructing a computer to perform accordingly. The chef-d'oeuvre of the three men is what they call a General Problem Solver, a set of instructions enabling the machine to behave "adaptively," to reason in terms of means and ends, to solve problems by first solving subproblems, and to "adjust aspiration to the attainable."

THE COMPUTER AND THE MANAGER

Regardless of what happens in heuristics, some computer men predict, jobs at the middle management level will become more specialized, specific, and highly programmed;

they will also become relatively fewer. On the other hand, managers at the top levels, freed of the need for analyzing details, will more than ever require the faculties of innovation, creativeness, and vision. The computer, precisely because it will make all relevant information instantly available to top management, will probably mean more centralization.

Such developments may well tend to humanize rather than dehumanize business. The company man, the Organization Man, will still exist, but only to the extent that he does or ever did exist. The kind of large-scale organization that the machine will encourage should stimulate personal initiative. At the average worker's level the computer, because it continually reports back on a job, is already improving his sense of personal participation. "Constant monitoring," says William Norris, founder and president of Control Data Corporation, which uses one of its own management systems, "makes employees feel part of the team effort, because their performance is judged without bias. We've found that people consequently upgrade their own performance."

Few men have speculated more boldly about the role of the computer in management than Herbert Simon. At the middle management level, he says, much time is now taken up with pacesetting, work pushing, and expediting. As decision making becomes automated and rationalized, these functions are likely to become less important. The manager will deal with well-structured problems, and will not have to spend so much time persuading, prodding, rewarding, and cajoling "unpredictable and sometimes recalcitrant people." Some managerial types, he allows, get a lot of satisfaction out of manipulating personal relationships; but he believes the diminution in general frustration, for middle managers as a group, will more than offset the other loss.

Heuristically programmed computers, Simon predicts, will be a long time surpassing men on jobs where they exercise their senses and muscles as well as their brains—i.e., running a bulldozer over rough ground, examining a piece of tissue in medical diagnosis, face-to-face service jobs, and so on. "Man has an advantage in rough environment," he explains. "Who would be easier to automate—the theoretical physicist or the experimental? The theoretical. The experimental physicist still has to cope with outside environment, whereas the theoretical one deals with concepts, ideas, and other inputs that have been highly processed."

Relative costs, Simon goes on, will decide who does the job; if a decision-making computer comes to $10,000 a month, it obviously might cost more than three middle managers. As yet, computers put to heuristic problem solving do not have anything remotely like the advantage over man that they boast in arithmetic and scientific computing. But the unit costs of using a computer are declining steadily.

"CHANGES HAVE GOT TO BE MADE"

Not everybody in the computer field is quite as sanguine as Simon about the machine's ability to substitute for human decision making, at any rate within the lifetime of most people. But the realization that the computer may be able to do a lot a man can do has accelerated the uproar in certain quarters about unemployment to panic proportions. Fevered by vague premonitions about the long-range consequences of the computer, many social pundits are discharging pneumatic predictions about how the machine will plow up the whole order. The consensus of a high-level symposium at a 1963 convention of the American Federation of Information Processing Societies seemed to be that the computer would be a large factor in making relatively full employment hard to achieve.

Most pessimistic of the lot was W. H. Ferry, vice-president of the Fund for the Republic, director of its Study of the Economic Order, and a man given to looking into the future farther than the human eye can see. It is Ferry's oft-stated thesis that the United States is caught on a horn of plenty, and that economic theories adequate to the old Industrial Revolution are no longer good enough. Since the individualism of the eighteenth and nineteenth centuries and "old theories of private property" are casualties of technology, Ferry argues, the complexity of the scientific-industrial state calls for more national planning. "Our sociopolitical thinking," said Ferry, "is still back in agrarian days. Changes have got to be made."

This kind of thinking, like King Lear's threats to do such things as "What they are, yet I know not, but they shall be the terrors of the earth," gets considerably ahead of the facts in the short run, and woefully distorts the possibilities over the long run. Social change is nothing new. In the main, social progress, as it is measured today, is a result of rising productivity, which was responsible for the fact that the proportion of American families with incomes of more than $4,000 (in "real" 1962 dollars) rose from 56 per cent in 1947 to 69 per cent in 1962. The critical question, obviously enough, is whether the computer will help accelerate the present rate of productivity growth so explosively that the economy will be unable to absorb people as fast as they are displaced.

Despite spectacular individual examples of the computer's ability to displace people, it seems to have had little effect on the nation's aggregate productivity—so far. Although productivity in the private economy grew at about 3.5 per cent annually in 1961–1963, against an average of 2.5 per cent in the seven previous years, similar spurts have occurred in the precomputer past. And what is often disregarded is that the economy is showing a gratifying ability to create jobs. It is true that U.S. manufacturing employment hardly increased at all in the four years 1960–1963, while manufacturing output rose 18 per cent; but in the same years other employment, despite a brace of rolling recessions, expanded enough to elevate total employment from about 65,600,000 to about 68,800,000. In 1963 alone, when rising productivity in effect subtracted about two million jobs from the economy, nonfarm wage and salary employment increased by more than 1,500,000. In other words, the economy in effect created a total of more than 3,500,000 jobs, and practically all were provided by private enterprise. *Fortune* magazine's economists estimate that if GNP rises to $650 billion (in late 1963 prices) by the middle of 1965, unemployment will be approaching "normal" levels, and the economy may absorb nearly all the employables. The unemployables, particularly the unskilled, will, of course, remain the problem.

The doomsday prophets ignore this. The moment of truth, they keep insisting, is still to come, and it will come all of a sudden. Their arguments run like this:

1. Computer applications have not yet affected national employment figures partly because their ability to displace people has been temporarily offset by more jobs in computer manufacturing and in new installations. Much heavy initial expense is charged to current account, which tends to hide the rate at which productivity improves. But soon the development phase will be over.

2. What intensifies the grim outlook is that the computer's great impact will come at a bad time. The labor force, owing

to the wartime baby boom, is increasing at a net rate of around a million a year, and by the end of the decade will increase by nearly two million a year. Largely as a result of computerized automation and cybernation, the number of blue-collar jobs is likely to increase little if at all; and one has only to look at the computer's successful routine applications to see what it may do to white-collar employment.

3. The computer indirectly spurs productivity. Not only does it make existing machines more productive, but it stimulates the purchase of newer and still more efficient machines, thus compounding its threat to employment.

MILLIONS OF NEW JOBS

These points are apposite and worth attention, and therein lies their potency in debate. But they are only one side of the story. Computers are not made out of thin air, and emphatically they do not operate unattended. The computer industry, including the infant "software" business of processing information for the computer, is employing more and more people. Paul Armer of Rand Corporation estimates that it will create a million new jobs in the next five years. Some say that by 1970 programming alone will employ 500,000.

The key factors are payoff and total investment. Just as the importance of any machine to the economy may be roughly gauged by the amount of capital invested in it, so its disemployment effect may be roughly gauged by the net return on that capital. In 1963, as already noted, U.S. government and industry bought or leased computers and accessory devices worth almost $2 billion, and in five years may be spending two or three times as much. These outlays are great, but they are a small part of the roughly $80 billion that industry and government invested in the private economy in 1964; five years from now they will still be a relatively small part of the money government and industry will be investing then.

Assume that computer users will eventually save a staggering 50 per cent annually on the capital value of their equipment, a margin the average user will not remotely approach for a long time. Five years hence, on annual hardware shipments valued at some $4 billion, they would earn some $2 billion, which could be equated with perhaps 200,000 fewer jobs. Or to be safe, double the number. But remember that in 1963 alone the economy in effect created a total of more than 3,500,000 jobs.

Such reckoning takes no account of the fact that the computer pervades so many activities and makes so much other capital equipment more productive. But the disemployment effect of all other plant and equipment, some of it automated and computerized, may also be measured roughly by its payoff. An uncontrollable upward surge in unemployment would necessarily be accompanied by a huge increase in payoff, and the expectation of the yield would be generating a colossal boom in capital spending. The steel industry is a case in point. It has far more than enough capacity, but it is spending huge sums on oxygen converters and automatic mills because it believes they will pay off handsomely. If all industry were anticipating similar returns, U.S. capital investment today would be vastly greater than it is.

THE TIMELY REPLENISHMENT

Too often forgotten is that machines over the years have not merely replaced men but have enabled them to do more or have freed them to do other things, and so have enlarged the economy's per capita production and the consumers' buying power and range of choices. Although it is sometimes hard to show just how displacement of man by the machine results in new jobs, it always has and always will. The computer will also help create new jobs. A computer-controlled oil refinery employs fewer people than a conventional refinery, but it helps bring costs and prices down; and a steady reduction in the real price of petroleum products helps increase the demand for them and so generates thousands of jobs in their distribution and sale. An automated plastics plant creates jobs for managers, engineers, salesmen, manufacturers, retailers. Sometimes, moreover, productivity increases are "hidden" in the form of a product's improved quality and utility. Thanks in part to computers in factories and offices, today's automobile is a much better car than previous models costing the same; thanks to computer-guided inventory controls, the consumer has a wider range of choice in cars than he has ever had before.

An overwhelming case could be made for the proposition that if the computer did not exist, it would have to be invented. Only a few years ago a good many economists were wondering whether U.S. productivity could keep on rising as it rose in the early postwar years, and some were skeptical when in 1959 *Fortune* projected an average annual increase of about 3 per cent for the 1960s. Their skepticism was hardly arbitrary. Ever since the original industrial revolution, the per capita growth rate of nations has been the result not of a single development but of a series of developments. As one innovation began to exhaust its power to multiply human effort, another came along. In several U.S. industries, notably agriculture, mining, and some manufacturing, there were portents of such exhaustion. In others featherbedding was (and still is) rife. The big question was not job displacement, but what would provide a new lift to the per capita growth rate. The answer to the question appears to be the computer. It will doubtless go down in history not as the explosion that blew unemployment through the roof, but as the technological triumph that enabled the American economy to maintain and gradually increase the secular growth rate on which its greatness depends.

2

"On Line" in "Real Time"

MEMBERS OF Westinghouse Electric Corporation's executive committee recently filed into a small room in the company's new Tele-Computer Center near Pittsburgh and prepared to look at their business as no group of executives had ever looked at business before. In front of them was a large video screen, and to one side of the screen was a "remote inquiry" device that seemed a cross between a typewriter and a calculator. As the lights dimmed, the screen lit up with current reports from many of the company's important divisions—news of gross sales, orders, profitability, inventory levels, manufacturing costs, and various measures of performance based on such data. When the officers asked the remote-inquiry device for additional information or calculations, distant computers shot back the answers in seconds.

This was only an experimental performance, designed to show how the corporation's decision makers could someday be provided with practically all the timely and relevant information they need to run the company. No computer system can do that yet, and it may be some time before men will be able to put enough consequential information in the machine to make it indispensable at high policy levels; but top managers in companies like Westinghouse are enthusiastically supporting the efforts of their computer men to convert common business data into useful knowledge.

Knowledge is power and control, provided it is timely, ample, and relevant. Only a businessman who knows what is happening inside his company reasonably soon after it happens can adjust his means to his aims; and only one who understands what is happening in the marketplace reasonably soon after it happens can really make sound decisions about his aims. But even a lot of timely facts is not enough. Most facts are either dead the moment they are born, or are the remnants of autopsies on history. Unless a man understands how they are related, and particularly how their relationships are changing, he knows very little.

Today's electronic computer enables a man to control his business and to assess its environment with incomparable effectiveness in two ways. (1) It enables him to lay hands on relevant facts swiftly; besides supplying him with facts in historical time, or after they have happened, it supplies him with facts "on line," i.e., as soon as they are born, and in "real time," i.e., promptly and abundantly enough to control the circumstances they describe while those circumstances are developing. (2) The computer helps the businessman understand the changing relationships of facts chiefly by a technique known as simulation, or the imitation of experience with models. Without the computer, he must build many models and compare them laboriously, or even construct pilot plants, and both methods are enormously expensive. With the computer he needs only to translate an appropriate number of models into mathematical formulas and instruct the computer to compare them and pick the likeliest. He can also simulate part or all of his operation in the machine, and test it in dozens of different situations.

The simulation technique grows in effectiveness when a corporation can repeatedly inspect its past performance and gauge its objectives accordingly—that is, after the business has become computerized, and the records of its transactions over the years have been stored in the machine's memory. Given such a continuum of information, the businessman can keep on refining his model by taking it apart, nailing down its variables, rejiggering its weights. As time passes, his model gets better and better, and he can make millions of telling comparisons in a few minutes. He knows precisely what has happened and why, what should be happening and why, and he has an excellent notion of what is likely to happen, and what is the best way of forfending or capitalizing on it all. He can rely less and less on guesses and hunch and more and more on analysis. As somebody once remarked hyperbolically, an executive is a genius if he is right 52 per cent of the time. Whatever the correct percentage, computer men argue, the machine can help him expand and elevate his native intuitive powers to new levels.

Most of the 13,000 computer installations used by U.S. business are assigned to routine data processing. But now that the practicality of real-time applications is being demonstrated, more and more corporations are starting the arduous process of putting themselves at least partly on real time lest competitors get the jump on them. By 1970, some computer sages predict, nearly all new electronic data-processing systems will be on line in real time. Just what this can mean to business can be demonstrated by close looks at three existing applications and a fourth whose potentials are still to be realized. The first is SABRE, American Airlines' long-awaited seat-reservation system, which is basically a highly ingenious method for keeping inventory in line. The second is Westinghouse Electric's steady progress in building up an integrated common data system. The third is Lockheed Missiles & Space's inexpensive and sophisticated system for controlling the costs of what was a complex and intractable production process. The fourth application is a kind of preview of real time on U.S. railroads, which are just beginning to sample the possibilities in the combination of computer, flanged wheel, and smooth rail.

BILLIONS FOR DEFENSE—AND EXPERIENCE

All these projects owe a great deal to the Air Force's SAGE. The acronym literally stands for Semi-Automatic Ground Environment, but it actually means the semi-automatic control of the basic environment in which the organization (here the Air Defense Command) does business, which is what every real-time system is about. As many know, SAGE was set up to protect the United States against surprise air attack. It does the job with a network of radar-fed computers that continuously analyze every cubic foot of air space around the United States, instantly track all airborne objects approaching the country, and call for appropriate action. M.I.T.'s Lincoln Laboratories, working with I.B.M. and Burroughs, took seven years to develop SAGE to the point where the first of its sixteen centers was completed in 1958; and System Development Corporation of Santa Monica, California, spent no fewer than 1,800 man-years writing SAGE's *original* programs. So far, the system has cost taxpayers some $1.6 billion, but it is teaching valuable business lessons as well as guarding the country.

One big lesson it teaches, aside from the fact that it puts the whole business on line in real time, is how to manage the symbiosis of man and machine. SAGE matches the two easily and naturally, letting the computer help rather than take over. The computer could be programmed to send up interceptors when it discovers something suspicious overhead; actually it notifies human monitors, who double-check with FAA and other authorities. If necessary, they in turn notify the Weapons Director, who decides whether to send up interceptor planes or even missiles. Although the computer itself can decide what and how many to send up and from what base, the Weapons Director usually asks the machine for several alternatives, from which he picks the best. Once a plane has taken off, the computer can infallibly guide the machine to its interception and back; all the human pilot needs to do is to take off, turn on his automatic pilot and gunsight, and land his craft. But he can and does override the computer.

Another lesson taught by SAGE lies in its practice of training Air Force officers in the use of computers. Not only are these officers constantly improving the capabilities and efficiency of the machines, they are learning more about the business of defending the nation than they could in any other way. If every management man knew as much about his business as the average SAGE officer does about his, it is fair to say that U.S. industry would be a lot more efficient than it is.

SAGE has probably taught more lessons about the art of simulation than any other computer installation; its great value indeed is that with it the Air Force keeps improving its ability to defend the country by simulating attacks in real time, and putting officers and pilots through their paces. In the command-and-control room the generals sit in a semicircle facing a huge luminous screen on which the computer displays the game in progress. Armed with light guns somewhat like Buck Rogers', they command the computer to deliver relevant information, to make calculations, and to suggest alternative courses. They analyze their mistakes and mull over their triumphs. Granted that SAGE has no budget worries in the usual sense of the phrase, and that it does not have to cope with the myriad variables that vex businessmen, it is probably the most edifying real-time pilot plant ever built.

A LIFT TO THE LOAD FACTOR

Without SAGE there would be no SABRE, at least not for a long time. SABRE, which is diagrammed in the accompanying chart, is American Airlines' $30-million real-time seat-reservation system, the foundation of its future integrated control system, and probably the most exasperatingly difficult civilian computer installation to date. Over ten years ago SABRE was spelled SABER because it then stood for Semi-Automatic Business Environment Research; today it is only a name suggesting speed and ability to hit the mark. At that time I.B.M., which was still up to its neck in SAGE, got together with American Airlines, and the two began to research A.A.'s problems. I.B.M. certainly has not put so many man-years into programming the project as System Development Corporation put into SAGE, but it put more into SABRE than it hoped to or cares to admit. More than eighty different actions are involved in making a reservation; the system contains more than a million instructions; and the specifications for its programs fill five thick volumes. Yet the time was well spent, for I.B.M. has acquired priceless knowledge.

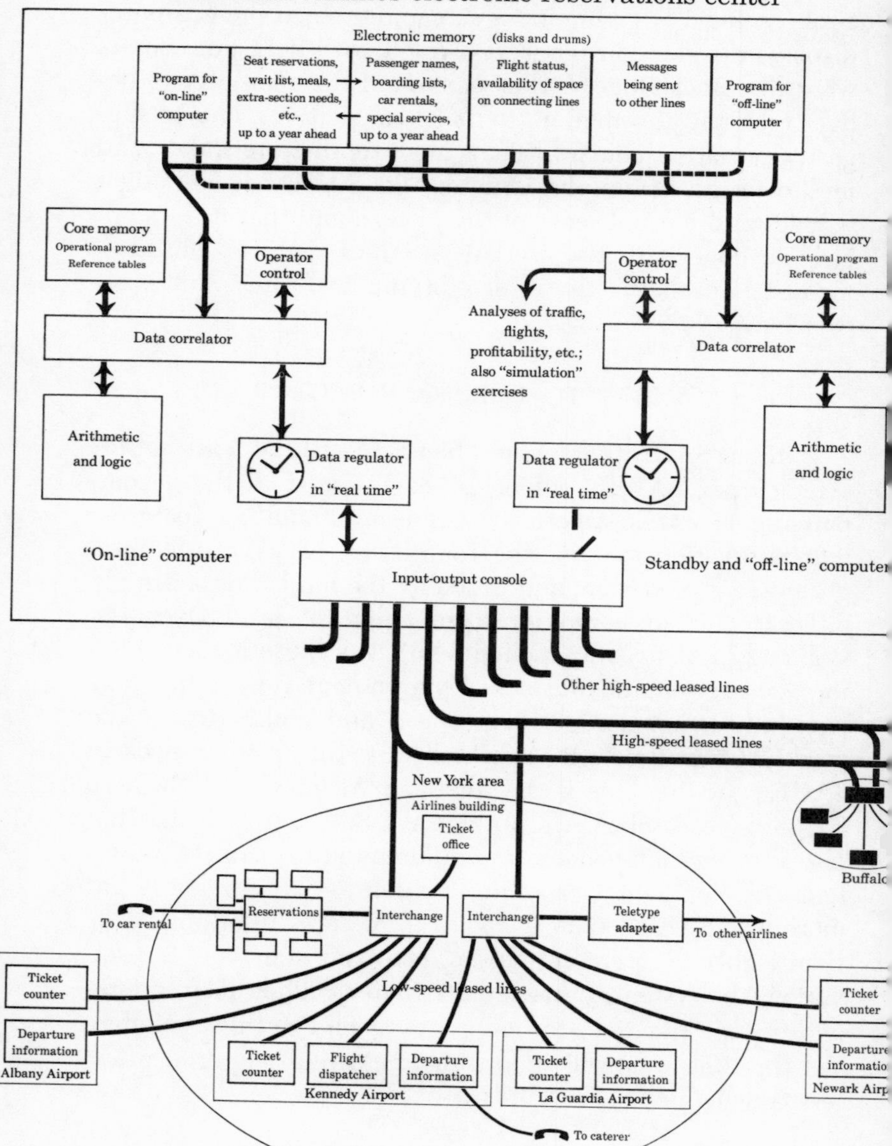
American Airlines electronic reservations center
Electronic memory (disks and drums)
Program for "on-line" computer
Seat reservations, wait list, meals, extra-section needs, etc., up to a year ahead
Passenger names, boarding lists, car rentals, special services, up to a year ahead
Flight status, availability of space on connecting lines
Messages being sent to other lines
Program for "off-line" computer
Core memory
Operational program
Reference tables
Operator control
Data correlator
Arithmetic and logic
Data regulator in "real time"
"On-line" computer
Analyses of traffic, flights, profitability, etc.; also "simulation" exercises
Input-output console
Standby and "off-line" computer
Other high-speed leased lines
High-speed leased lines
New York area
Airlines building
Ticket office
Reservations
To car rental
Interchange
Interchange
Teletype adapter
To other airlines
Low-speed leased lines
Ticket counter
Departure information
Albany Airport
Ticket counter
Flight dispatcher
Departure information
Kennedy Airport
Ticket counter
Departure information
La Guardia Airport
To caterer
Ticket counter
Departure information
Newark Airp
Buffalo

I. SABRE, A $30-MILLION APPLICATION

In the two and one-half seconds between the last word of a would-be passenger's request for space and the first word of the agent's reply, a $30-million computer operation has not only booked him on the correct flight as far as a year ahead but, once it gets his name, will keep track of his every move along the line—including ordering his meals, his rental cars, or his connecting reservations—until he arrives where he wants to go.

SABRE, built for American Airlines by I.B.M., is the largest commercial real-time data-processing system in operation. And unlike previous airline reservation systems, it is alpha-numeric; that is, it handles and correlates names and numbers. As flight and passenger data are punched or typed, they are turned into electronic "bits," the basic form of computer information, and fed by regular leased telephone lines to a nearby Interchange or "Buffer," which transmits a complete message to the SABRE center in Westchester County, New York.

At SABRE the Input-Output Console "polls" each interchange station for messages on a split-second basis. The data travels from Interchange to Console over special high-speed A.T.&T. lines. The Console then routes it to the one of two I.B.M. 7090 computers that is currently "On Line" (*left*) while the Standby (*right*), ready to cut in instantly if needed, goes about special problems fed in by the local operator. At the Data Regulator incoming bits of characters are checked for sense and accuracy, and then assembled into six-character (thirty-six bit) "words" for computer use.

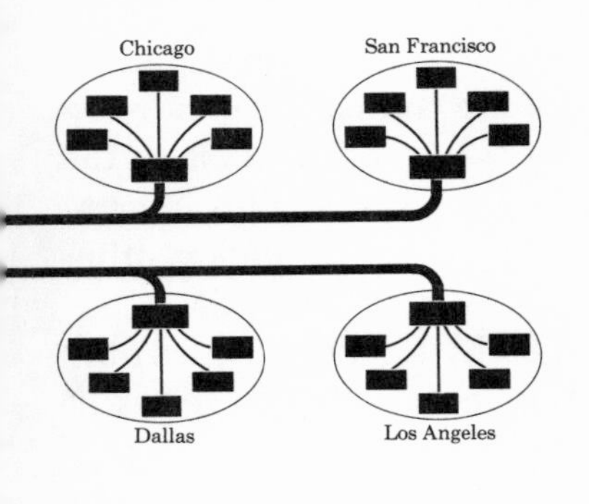

The rest of the boxes shown in the diagram are schematic elements of the computer operation: the Arithmetic and Logic section provides any computations required before or after information passes into the memory units. Core Memory is the brain, holding the "programs" that direct the entire operation. But SABRE is far more than a lightninglike bookkeeper; it is also a stern controller: if the agent forgets any details, it reminds him. Because it forfends duplicate bookings under a misspelled name and returns canceled seats immediately to inventory SABRE eventually will enable the airlines virtually to eliminate the "no-show" problem.

Seat reservations may seem a trifling problem, and SAGE officers sometimes dismiss SABRE as the kids' SAGE. But in an economic sense the most important and difficult problem in running an airline is not flying planes but handling the inventory of seats. The problem gets worse as traffic increases; not only has the cost of handling each customer's request for space risen faster than revenues, so has the difficulty in keeping up the occupancy rate or load factor. Nothing is more important to an airline. Unless a certain percentage of its seats are occupied by flight time, it flies for broke. The difference between profit and loss is very small, often no more than the difference between a load factor of 50 and 55 per cent. But making money is not a simple matter of selling a few more seats on each flight. Some 40 per cent of American Airlines' traffic is on flights that are technically sold out twenty-four hours before departure; actually they are rarely sold out. For various reasons, including "no-shows," they are lucky to depart 90 per cent full. Since every sale that raises this percentage is almost pure profit, raising it makes an enormous difference in the company's final reckoning. If anybody cancels a seat anywhere on the system the company ideally should be able to offer it a second later to somebody else anywhere on the system. This, among other things, is what SABRE does.

Fully operating since late 1964, SABRE should be earning 30 per cent or more on its investment—and that in terms of staff savings. Other benefits will accrue, e.g., the load factor will be much higher than it would be otherwise. And the standby computer will be used for other computing and simulation. Eventually SABRE will probably be integrated with the company's other installations, such as the machine that now helps figure out flight plans at a saving of about $2 million a year.

THIRTY PER CENT PAYOFF FOR WESTINGHOUSE

Westinghouse Electric Corporation is said to use computers in a wider range of applications than any other U.S. company; whether it does or not, it has a clear notion of what it wants to do with them. The aim of the company's business-systems department, says Lou Hague, its director, is to shrink the lead time in the management information cycle to practically nothing, and eventually to be able to prepare a final report that will include just about everything top management needs to make its decisions. A few are skeptical. In the March–April 1964 issue of the *Harvard Business Review,* John Dearden of the Harvard Business School contended that the computer may be great for controlling operations, but most of top management's decisions are not concerned with operations, and therefore flooding it with operational information is "sheer nonsense." Computer systems people, including Hague, reply that no competent systems man proposes to inundate managers with useless information, and anyway no good manager would stand for it. The phrase for what they want to present to top management is "exception information," or information that demands attention and action. Moreover, they believe that the computer can and increasingly will provide top management with information indispensable for strategic planning, and that the progressive, smart top manager will encourage his systems men in their efforts to bring such information to him.

How the computer monitors exception information at Westinghouse is illustrated by an example the business-systems department uses for internal education. Costs in a certain plant have been normal for a while, but begin to rise steeply. Without the computer, these costs would get far out of line before being noticed, and would not be brought back for a week or more; but with real-time control they get only a little out of line before being noticed, and are brought back promptly. The cumulative effect on profits can be enormous.

Westinghouse's business-systems department is tackling one problem at a time; Hague says it does not yet know enough to do the job all at once, and he doubts that anyone else does. And the company keeps expansion within realistic limits by making computer operations pay off in identifiable savings. In 1963 Westinghouse spent $16,200,000 for machine rentals and programming and research. But it realized $20,700,000 and thus saved $4,500,000 or nearly 30 per cent on its outlays, not including indirect benefits such as better customer service and improved cash flow.

Westinghouse's adventure with the computer began in the late 1950s, when Hague hired James Emery, now teaching management information systems at M.I.T., to tackle the problem of adjusting inventory supply to demand in the transformer plant at Sharon, Pennsylvania. The job only sounds easy. Inventories of distribution transformers, which are mass produced, had a habit of piling up unless demand was estimated correctly. Emery and his associates resorted to simulations of demand based on such things as historical buying cycles, abnormal regional growth, and interest-rate levels. They fed the data into an I.B.M. 705, which forecast demand by size, type, and location. Thus simulating demand on a weekly basis, they sharply reduced inventories while giving customers better service. "We replaced a lot of discussion over the conference table with the computer," says Hague. "If we had known years before what we learned in 1958, we would have saved millions."

"A REAL SHOCKER AT TIMES"

Donald Burnham, now the president of Westinghouse, but then manufacturing vice president, was enthusiastic about the computer experiment from the start. In 1960, owing to his support, the business-systems department was founded, and plans were made for the Tele-Computer Center. Inventory control is now only part of a large-scale simulation operation that relates factory operation to buying patterns. At the Tele-Computer Center two Sperry Rand Univac 490s link 360 offices, factories, and warehouses in real time. They handle an average of 2,000 orders a day. They prepare invoices and bookkeep all transactions, and they send incoming orders to the nearest warehouse, and pick the next nearest warehouse if (as is unlikely) the nearest is out of the item they are looking for. Because they automatically adjust warehouse stocks to optimum level by sending a reorder to the factory, they have enabled the company to close six of its twenty-six warehouses and to slash inventories by roughly 35 per cent, as well as to provide better service.

Like many commercial real-time installations, this one uses a standby computer to take over if the on-line machine fails. The standby computer solves engineering problems, turns out payrolls and annual-report figures, pays dividends, and prepares various financial and sales data. This sort of chore, however, can also be done by the on-line computer. Handed an urgent query, say one asking if there is a left-handed pink refrigerator in stock, the on-line computer interrupts its routine duties to answer the question or even to make out an order and appropriately adjust inventory. But then it goes right back to the routine job it was doing.

Simulation is a standard procedure at Westinghouse. In scheduling its work, for example, the management of the

South Philadelphia turbine plant draws up dozens of alternative plans. Given the plans plus the actual orders on hand and the sequence in which they must be filled, the computer runs through the equivalent of two or three years of operation, and so helps decide on the best schedule. "It often only verifies our hunches," says Hague. "But it can be a real shocker at times." Simulation is also being used to evaluate plant sites and appraise other capital investment, but the most effective use of the technique will occur after more activities or "transactions" have been put on real time.

Westinghouse is now augmenting order and inventory control with production control. In its Elmira, New York, electronic-tube plant and in its South Philadelphia turbine plant the company is installing electronic data-gathering equipment that keeps accurate and timely records of various stages of production; Westinghouse estimates that such systems will pay off at 50 per cent.

While all this is going on, the business-systems department keeps its eye on the goal: shrink the management information cycle. To this end it has developed what it claims is a unique technique for retrieving information from a computer's memory. So-called random-access devices, which are standard peripheral equipment, enable a man to retrieve specific facts. But when he wants to find *all* the relevant information on a given subject, random-access devices do not help much. Business Systems' solution to the problem, oversimplified considerably, is to instruct the computer to file information under dozens of different headings, and then to use a "list processor" to retrieve the information by scanning appropriate categories serially. Suppose, for example, an official wants to find out how many Westinghouse people working in cryogenics have done graduate work at M.I.T. Working against three variables, the computer would have to labor through the whole random-access file to come up with the answer. But using the processor, it is back with the reply in twelve minutes: two out of 117,000 employees.

LOCKHEED ASKS ADA

As one of the world's leaders in aircraft and aerospace manufacturing, Lockheed began to use computers in the early 1950s for such jobs as calculating trajectories and designing space and other airborne vehicles. At the same time it set up a headquarters systems-planning department under Norman Ream, formerly an I.B.M. executive. In 1963 Lockheed's total computer rental was $17 million, and it employed 600 programmers, 160 system planners, and 1,350 data processors. The company's Missiles & Space Division has acquired considerable reputation for developing management games that simulate the business environment of the space industry; management teams represent imaginary competitive companies whose decisions are weighed by an appropriately instructed I.B.M. 7094.

In 1958 the Missiles & Space Division began to look for a system that could monitor and control its production, which accounts for nearly 40 per cent of the company's total employment. This operation, at first glance, seems the most unrewarding place in the world for a computer. Unlike repetitive mass production, which lends itself to standardized, methodical controls, the plants at Sunnyvale and Van Nuys, California, are massive job-shop operations. They simultaneously machine and otherwise alter and assemble 40,000 to 60,000 different items that range from electronic microscopic devices to space vehicles such as the Agena D, all with different completion schedules.

Nevertheless, Lockheed saw an opportunity to put the

computer to good use on this vexatious production problem. In the fast-changing aerospace world, the specifications of many jobs are modified after they are well along in the production process; merely to keep track of this bewildering sequence of variables required a staff of more than 600 expediters, and sometimes the best of them would take a day or two to find a part whose specifications had been changed. Precisely because the manufacturing processes and output were so various, in other words, Lockheed decided a real-time system could both reduce costs and control production with more dispatch. After a year of analysis, Lockheed called in R.C.A., which had begun to make electronic data-gathering equipment that could be hooked together by ordinary telephone wires and coupled with computers and random-access memories. The result was Lockheed's System ADA, for Automatic Data Acquisition.

What happens in ADA is that every part or piece of material arriving at the plant is immediately inventoried in the computer's memory, and from then until it leaves the plant its movements are recorded. As soon as the item is taken from inventory, and whenever it is worked on, an employee inserts a card into one of the 260 input stations scattered around the plants. Thus the computer always knows where the piece is, who is working on it, and what the job costs in wages. The computer also watches every piece in stock and reorders common items according to the number in current use—in other words, instead of simply counting, it makes judgments about the rate of use and so behaves heuristically.

Some of the returns so far:

• ADA has cost some $2,300,000 to develop. But by the end of 1964 it was paying off at more than $2 million or around 90 per cent annually. The chief reason for the high yield is that ADA eliminated 400 expediters and 200 clerks (owing to the company's high labor turnover, all who wanted to stay have been absorbed). Other kinds of companies, particularly those already using sophisticated batch systems, are manifestly not likely to realize such a return.

- ADA has rationalized supervisory functions. Under the old system the supervisors tended to iron out peaks and valleys in the work load over the week, and so to conceal the real daily output and capacity of their departments. Now that management knows precisely how long it takes to do every job and how much a department can do on any given day, its scheduling can be "optimized."
- ADA has been enthusiastically accepted by employees, who feel that they are reporting directly to higher management and bypassing the often prejudiced judgment of the supervisor. Interesting psychological note: the early input machines recorded employees' cards silently and left them with misgivings; now all the input machines click audibly when scanning cards.
- ADA enables management to locate work in progress instantly. Since engineering changes are constantly being made, this ability is highly valuable beyond the money it saved in eliminating expediters.
- ADA can analyze costs instantly, tell what machines are being utilized how much of the time for whose work, and so on. Thus ADA is being used to forecast manpower and plant needs.
- ADA, because it contains complete records of costs and quality of goods purchased in the past, allows purchasing agents to make quick, perceptive decisions on where and what to buy. In other words, the system keeps inventories of materials and supplies not only at optimum levels, but at optimum costs.

The new system developed some growing pains; in the

summer of 1962 it had to be suspended a month. The central equipment was being fed so much information and being asked for so many answers that it got some of the questions and answers confused. But this confusion was cleared up by minor alterations; and the system, though it is now four times as large as it was then, is functioning flawlessly. Lockheed has found so many new applications for the special information the system is generating that it called in Computer Sciences Corporation, one of the swiftly growing new firms specializing in systems and programming, to help it formulate new manufacturing and procurement status programs.

The system actually relieves top management of a lot of unnecessary detail. As Herschel Brown, executive vice-president of the Missiles & Space Division, puts it, one of the objectives of a computerized operation is to compress data—in other words, to provide only exception information—and this ADA does. Eventually, moreover, it will be part of an integrated management control system.

THE OL & RT RAILROAD

In few industries has the on-line, real-time principle a more stupendously promising application than on railroads. In the semi-automatic combination of flanged and tapered wheel and steel rail, railroads embodied the concepts of cybernation and automation a hundred years before their time; and the combination still gives them the power to move a ton a mile using less energy than any other form of transportation. An easy way to sense the potentialities of the computerized railroad is to think of it as a model system set up in the basement of a house. The system is on line in real time; the operator sees everything, knows everything, runs everything. With the help of computers, railroad managers could control 50,000-mile systems with the same quasi-omniscience exercised by the model railroader.

But for the railroad industry, control is more than a game. Although it has improved efficiency greatly since World War II, it must improve it more. Luckily, it has direct control over an extraordinarily large percentage of its costs. Although no other industry needs so much plant and equipment to generate a dollar of revenue (nearly $3 worth), few if any pay out so much of their revenues in wages (roughly 50 cents out of $1), and few if any spend so little of their revenues on outside materials and supplies (15 cents out of $1).

Nothing can help railroads haul down these costs more decisively than the computer. As yet, the 101 Class I railroads together own or lease only about a hundred machines, and nearly all are in controllers' offices. But several lines have recently decided to broaden their applications. The Southern Pacific, Atlantic Coast Line, Southern, and Louisville & Nashville are setting up I.B.M. systems to improve car usage. Western Pacific is working with General Electric's computer division, which is striving hard to make a big place for itself in several fields, and hopes to be one of the first carriers on a real-time basis.

Although rail executives do not have to know everything that happens the very moment it happens, the real-time concept is nevertheless supremely valid. "With our present reporting," says one railroad vice-president, "we can lose money for thirty days before we know it." Like many a non-transportation company, at least one railroad has saved money just by studying a computer system. Forced to redefine its functions, it has already eliminated a million dollars' worth of duplications, bottlenecks, and superfluous reports. As the Westinghouse and Lockheed experience suggests, shrinking the railroad management-information cycle should also pay off spectacularly.

Any attempt to computerize a railroad begins with the freight car, the unit expression of what the company has to sell and the biggest single item in its capital outlays. The average freight car produces (i.e., rolls) only 4 to 6 per cent of the time, or less than fifty miles a day, mainly because nobody knows where it is in time to use it efficiently. A 25 per cent improvement in utilization could save railroads up to $100 million a year.

The computer will increase utilization by putting every car on line in real time, just as it does every piece of work in Lockheed's Sunnyvale plant. It will order a car from the so-called car distributor, notify yardmasters to spot the car, send out waybills, record train departure, notify the yardmaster at the other end of the run where to spot the car, and make out bills and record payments. With all this on file, it will also forecast and plan car movements, dispatch cars to customers promptly, and handle instantly customers' requests for diversion, holding, expediting, and plain information. In short, it will cut costs while improving service. And because it will cover the whole railroad, it will provide the foundation for an integrated real-time system.

The computer will reduce other capital outlays or make them more productive. Railroads probably could save millions by judicious investment in modern earth-moving techniques for reducing curvature and grades. Although they have been making such simple calculations as how much more crude energy it takes to haul say 5,000 tons up a 1.5 per cent grade than up a 1 per cent grade, they have been unable to make complex calculations that take into account many factors like lost time and wheel wear. The computer can do so either by simulation or by straight calculation, and it may surprise if not shock the carriers with estimates of what line revision can save. It will also help them to judge and time outlays for other capital expenditures more efficiently.

THE INTEGRATED YARDMASTERS

Having attained much better car use, the computer will then help reduce other costs sharply. Less than half the average railroad's expenses go to roll trains over the line. The bulk goes into terminal operations—i.e., taking apart and assembling trains and maintaining classification yards, sidings, customers' tracks, etc. Here again the computer can reduce costs while improving service. Freight trains, except when laden with cargoes moving long distances in whole trainloads, are still pushed along from one yard to another. Every yardmaster clears his tracks as fast as he can, and the fact that the next yard may be in no position to handle cars efficiently bothers him not a bit. What he does not know does not concern him. But the computer will enable officers to run the railroad as a single unit; knowing what cars are moving where, they can tell every yardmaster just which cars to switch, which to hold, which to expedite. Because the yardmaster too will know what he is expected to do, he can use fewer switching crews and engines.

The computer will eventually be responsible for what one railroad man delicately calls a "restructuring" of his entire organization. It will save countless clerical man-hours. It will replace dispatchers, the functionaries who direct train movements by issuing orders to train crews. And it can replace most road engine and train crews. There is no technical reason at all why trains cannot be started, stopped, spaced, accelerated, decelerated, and otherwise operated by the computer, just as they are now kept on line by the flanged wheel. The passenger trains of the new San Francisco Bay Area Rapid Transit Line, operating up to eighty miles an hour as few as ninety seconds apart, will be run, separated, and regulated by a G.E. computer. Without a computer, as a matter of fact, the Bay Area line as now envisioned would be impossible. For other U.S. railroads to go on assigning a half-dozen or more men to a train will soon make no more sense than for General Motors to deploy regiments of repair men with monkey wrenches on its assembly lines.

The computer will operate trains much better and more safely than men can; not only will there be fewer enginemen or trainmen to get hurt in a wreck, there will be far fewer wrecks. The computer is not subject to man failure, and railroads will have the money to protect grade crossings and maintain their equipment and track better than they do now. Above all, the machine will make trains faster and more flexible. In order to keep down crew costs, which add up to around $1.25 a train-mile, railroads now hook as many as 200 cars behind several diesel units. Both service and speed suffer. With few crew costs to worry about, they can tailor the load to a single power unit, and again provide vastly better service at much lower cost. The problem ahead of the carriers is not technical but political; if the trouble they have had in revising obsolete work rules is any indication, the computerized automation of freight trains will take time, to say the least. But if the rails are to hold their own against competitors that are also computerizing, they have no choice but to automate trains.

THE GREAT SIMULATORS

The computer will enable the railroads to behave more like free enterprisers in other ways. They are now bound to the ball and chain of an obsolete rate structure that makes little attempt to relate costs and prices. Because railroad unit costs drop steeply as volume rises, nobody in the old days could figure out what it cost them to haul anything. As monopolies, therefore, railroads found it easy to charge what the traffic would bear, and they built up a value-of-service rate structure that later became a sitting duck for competitors who cut rates selectively on the high-valued traffic. The computer will enable railroads to estimate costs accurately, and make a far more convincing case for justified rate reductions before the ICC than they can now.

Since most of their problems are operational, railroads will find good use for a command and control system. This does not mean that officers will only have to sit around in a dimly lighted room, smoking big black cigars and watching a video screen. Like other businessmen, they will not want to be deluged with routine information; they too will want only exception information. But they will necessarily be great users of simulation. They will make hundreds of different assumptions and combinations of assumptions about such factors as traffic, schedules, train weight and speed, rates, and capital investment, and test each combination in the computer. Simulating years of railroading under widely different conditions, they will both achieve new levels of efficiency and service and develop the confidence to compete forcefully and imaginatively.

3

Machines That Man Can Talk With*

PERHAPS THE MOST STRIKING single fact about the continuing computer revolution is that the proudest achievements of today's machines will seem crude and primitive within a decade. Computers that spot errors in the instructions they are given (and type out reprimands), computers that transform rough drawings into finished engineering diagrams, computers that recognize handwriting and understand English—these are some of the new developments currently under active investigation.

They are a response to an urgent need for computers that are intelligent enough to be approached in a more democratic, "man to man" manner. Present-day computers have to be ordered about like menials. The user writes out a detailed program of instructions for them and then waits while the machine grinds out answers. This procedure is adequate for solving relatively straighforward problems, such as analyz-

* The author of this chapter is John Pfeiffer.

ing election returns or keeping inventories, where the investigator generally starts with a fairly precise idea of the information he needs.

But when he wants to do original work—say, to design a new space vehicle or devise a subtler business or military strategy—he cannot spell out step-by-step programs in advance. He must be able to maintain give-and-take relations with the computer instead of giving it peremptory commands. In other words, he must be able to talk easily with it, ask it questions, receive prompt replies, and change his mind at a moment's notice in the light of those replies. Communication at such a level calls for cleverer computers. So the emphasis of the most advanced development work is on designing new reading and writing and listening devices and, even more important, on new kinds of programs written in new languages. Although progress has been made in recent years, there is still a formidable language barrier between computers and their users. Conversations still tend to be a bit on the awkward side. As a rule, instructions are written in number codes or in hybrids composed of English words and special symbols. Many investigators would prefer to express themselves to the computer in a language somewhat closer to ordinary English. And they may soon be able to do so.

Close man-machine collaboration, of course, implies that the investigator will find a computer ready and willing to work with him whenever he wants assistance. But that may not always be so simple as it seems. The demand for computer time is increasing at such a rapid rate that some recently installed machines which were supposed to handle all needs for the next five years are already swamped. Under such heavy traffic conditions it would be impractical for one man to tie up one large computer for hours. To help alleviate this situation, considerable research is being devoted to the possibility of making the machines available to many investigators simultaneously, a development that may lead to radically new ways of using and marketing thinking power.

These are some of the main ideas behind a broad research drive that was launched in the fall of 1962. The drive is heavily supported by the Defense Department's farseeing Advanced Research Projects Agency. It is being led by some of the nation's foremost computer scientists and engineers at Carnegie Tech, M.I.T., Stanford, System Development Corporation, the University of California at Berkeley and Los Angeles, and the University of Pittsburgh. They are engaged in a long and arduous process of upgrading computers—of transforming glorified menials into equals, or at least potential equals.

Chapter 2 described some of the more exciting applications of current computer technology. This chapter focuses attention on certain outstanding research projects that promise to have a notable future impact on every area of science and technology. The payoff is likely to be spectacular, for recent investigations seem to have a self-accelerating quality. Every new advance enhances our ability to design machines that will speed the coming of further advances.

One of the most striking new developments is "Sketchpad," the "robot draftsman," which is described in this chapter. Engineers discussing design problems tend to think on paper, expressing their ideas in the form of rough sketches or block diagrams. Sketchpad enables them to work in roughly the same way with the TX-2 computer, a pioneer machine developed at M.I.T.'s Lincoln Laboratory. The TX-2 becomes, among other things, a fast and extraordinarily versatile draftsman.

Using Sketchpad, an engineer designing a new mechanical

arrangement can see how it will perform without building a model. The new graphical system can do things that no human draftsman has been able to do up to now. The machine can be ordered to animate the drawing, to make the parts rotate at high speeds or in slow motion, so that their linkages may be studied in action. It is also possible for an engineer to draw a bridge and tell the machine to compute stresses at specified beams, to "animate" electric-circuit diagrams to show how currents flow through them, and to perform a variety of other operations.

TÊTE-À-TÊTE WITH TX-2

The most exciting thing about the system is that it illustrates the enormous power of an effective man-computer combination. A young computer engineer, Ivan Sutherland, is responsible for Sketchpad. He invented it in 1961 to fulfill his requirements for a doctor's degree, and finished his part of the project about eighteen months later. (Sketchpad is only a beginning, but is being intensively explored and extended by other investigators.)

The fundamental point is that Sutherland would never have developed Sketchpad if he had worked under the conditions prevailing in the conventional computer center. The way things are generally run is that an investigator starting fresh on a brand-new problem prepares a preliminary program in the form of a deck of punch cards, and brings it to the computer room. From there on in he and his program are quickly parted. Instructions are fed into the machine, which stands in shining isolation, often on display behind glass doors and glass walls like a custom-built yacht, lights flashing and reels of magnetic memory tape spinning. The computer can probably handle the problem in minutes or seconds. But

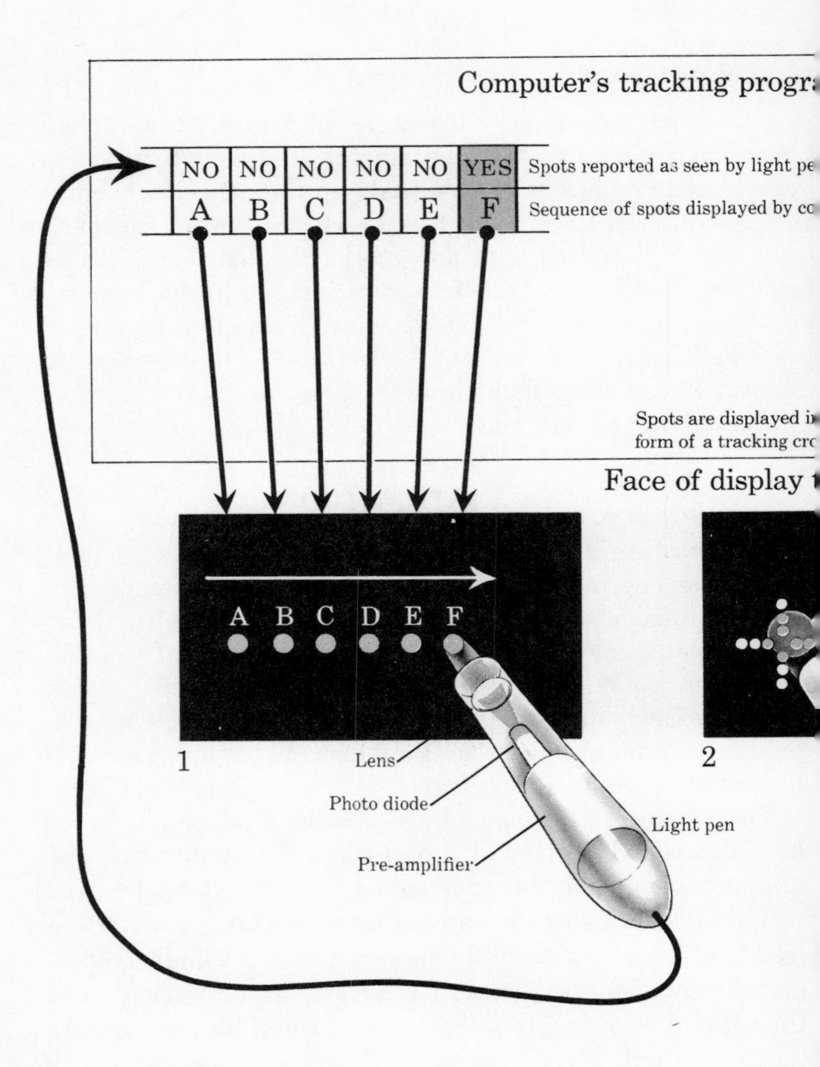

II. THE ROBOT DRAFTSMAN

A major breakthrough in the art of communicating with computers is Sketchpad, developed by Ivan Sutherland at M.I.T.'s Lincoln Laboratory. Sketchpad makes it possible to use the face of a TV-type display tube like a sheet of paper, on which sketches can be drawn with a light sensitive pen or electronic stylus. An operator draws on a Sketchpad display tube mounted on the console of the laboratory's

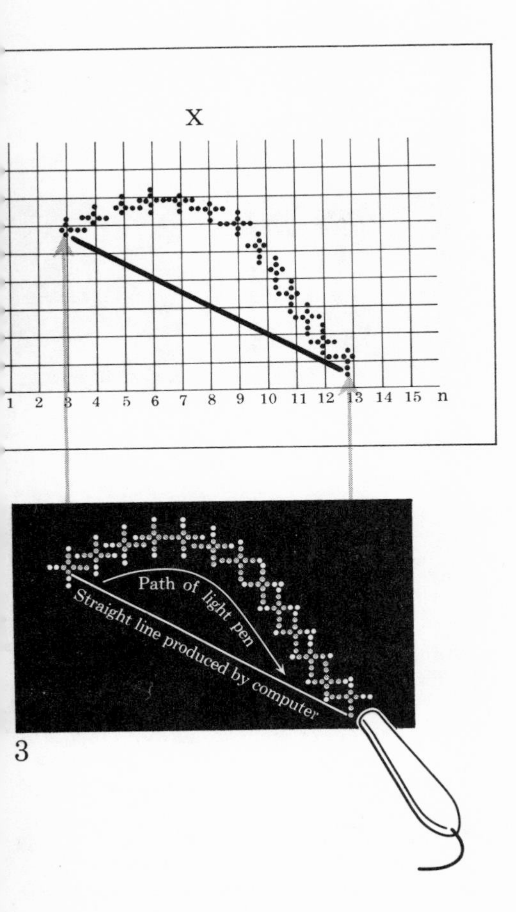

TX-2 computer. The pen contains an electric eye that responds to bright spots which appear on the tube (*see diagram 1*) in the form of tiny tracking crosses (*diagram 2*). When the pen is moved along just above the tube's surface, a glowing fluorescent line forms. Freehand sloppiness is automatically transformed into neat lines. The machine, having been instructed beforehand by the pressing of the proper push button, "knows" that a straight line is called for—and creates one no matter how much the hand wavers (*diagram 3*). (*Cont. next page*)

How to draw a hexagon

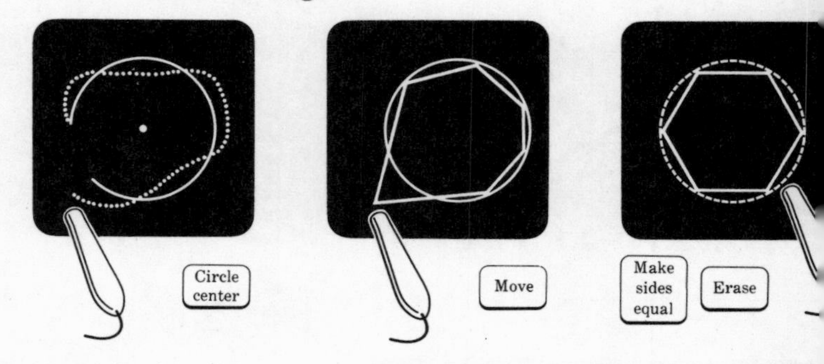

(*Cont. from preceding page*) Similarly, Sketchpad will produce a perfect circle, as indicated in the first step of the sequence showing how a hexagon may be drawn. When the hexagon is roughly sketched, the computer promptly produces a regular geometric figure. Once the hexagon (or any other form) has been completed, it can be moved, reduced, or enlarged up to 2,000 times, duplicated and rotated by operating appropriate toggle switches and push buttons.

The Animated Blueprint illustrates one Sketchpad feature that is expected to find widespread industrial application. Ordinarily, when human draftsmen want to modify a drawing, they must redraw the whole thing. Electronic draftsmen, however, work faster and more directly. In the Sketchpad system it is sufficient merely to point at part of the drawing with the light pen and indicate how it should be changed. The computer then does the required redrawing according to the new specifications, and indicates the changes in four different projections.

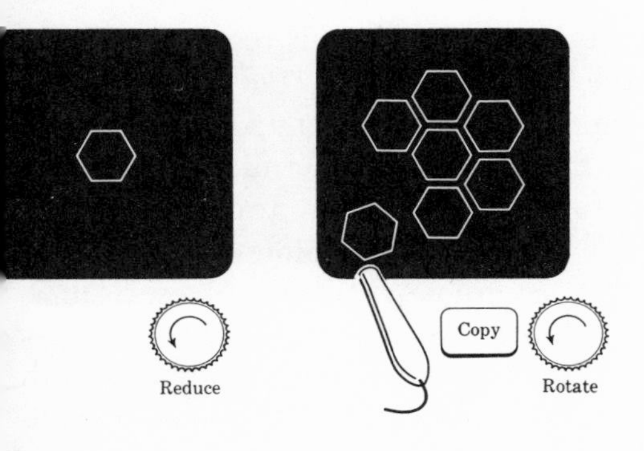

›nimated blueprint

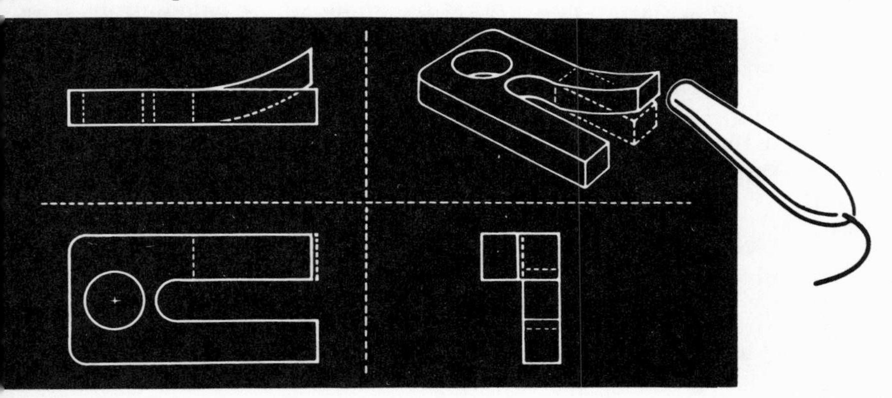

it is booked in advance, and during a busy day it may handle several hundred individual jobs. So the investigator has to wait from three to twenty-four hours for his results, an interruption that hardly promotes concentrated study.

The TX-2, on the other hand, was designed specifically to "give the game back to the players"—to permit intimate and continued association of man and machine. Investigators use it on an informal "tennis court" basis, signing up for periods during which they have it completely to themselves. Sutherland sat at a console, relayed instructions to the TX-2 by teletypewriter, and watched what happened as he drew with the light pen. He arranged things so that the machine informed him about its current "thoughts," typing back messages which indicated what it was doing at any given moment. By reading these messages and observing events on the screen, he could tell when the TX-2 was involved in a "loop" (that is, performing the same set of calculations over and over again) and, if so, whether the operation was producing desired results. He could even hear the machine talking to itself, recognizing loops and other operations by characteristic pulsings and squeals and whines. Sutherland has felt the strange excitement of such work: "It's like flying a jet plane. You have a machine that can do a lot for you if you treat it right. I spent hours with it, at times when there was no one to interrupt me, and it was a thrill to struggle with an idea and then to see it working on the screen."

Just what is new about Sketchpad? Not the TX-2, which has been engaged in fancy problem-solving for more than five years. Not the light pen, a device developed some fifteen years ago for use in the SAGE air-defense system. Not the memory units or logical circuits or any of the other things that are collectively known in the computer business as "hardware." What makes Sketchpad unique is its "software," the instructions Sutherland has fed into the computer.

To an appreciable extent the computer revolution has become a revolution in software. Given a good machine, a system of suitably assembled electronic parts, everything depends on how it is used and what is put into it. In a sense, a computer represents an unrealized potential, something to be shaped by man's ideas. Roughly speaking, software is for a computer what education is for a child.

An outstandingly well-educated computer is the I.B.M. 7094 machine housed at the Watson Research Center in Yorktown Heights, New York. For one thing, it provides vivid proof of the fact that a properly programmed machine can learn and learn well enough to surpass its human programmer. Arthur Samuel, consultant to I.B.M.'s director of research, has taught it not only to play checkers but also to improve its game. Even when it was first described in *Fortune* ("Problems, Too, Have Problems," October, 1961), the computer could beat Samuel handily, and it enjoyed a high amateur status. Now it has advanced to tournament class. When it played six games with Robert Nealey, Connecticut state champion, it compiled a record of one loss and five draws, which is bad news for any non-electronic opponents who may be foolhardy enough to challenge it in another year or two.

JOHNNIAC CORRECTS THE TEACHER

It is a somewhat humbling fact that even today's comparatively uneducated computers are less prone to make mistakes than the people who use them. Indeed, human fallibility is one of the major obstacles to effective employment of computers. We can get an idea of the difficulty by visiting an average computer center where deliver-and-wait procedure is the rule. The investigator brings his preliminary program to the computer room, and hours later receives his results—but they are almost certainly *not* the answers he wants. The odds are that the machine has rejected his program because some of the instructions contained errors. A man can understand a telegram bringing "HAPP BIRTHDAY" greetings or a menu offering a "Spannish omelet and cole, slaw" or a newspaper report describing a "crisis int he Far East." But most machines are nonplussed by such errors.

So the investigator must start "debugging," the long and tedious process of finding and correcting the mistakes he has made. Then he brings the revised program to the computer room and waits again, only to learn that there are still errors. This frustrating process may be repeated many times. A moderate-sized program, say a program designed to handle part of a weather-forecasting problem, may consist of 20,000 instructions to start with and half as many more in its final fully edited form. Developing the program probably requires 150 to 300 separate runs on the computer (an average of seven to ten bad runs for every good one), six months of work, and a total of six hours of actual calculating time. Most of the time is used for refining and debugging; only fifty minutes or so are devoted to obtaining the solution of the problem.

The entire situation has the nightmarish quality of a telephone conversation with a ten-hour delay between remarks. Suppose a housewife reads a list of items to her grocer early Monday morning and does not hear from him until shortly before dinner time, when he tells her: "Sorry. I didn't understand something you said near the beginning of your list." So she checks back and reads the list again. Assuming no further difficulties crop up, her order should be delivered Tuesday morning. If there were no other way of getting food, she would adjust to such a routine and be thankful. A comparable situation prevails in today's computer centers.

When investigators work directly with computers face to face, as it were, the situation will be more like a normal telephone call. Mistakes can be taken care of on the spot and delays reduced to a minimum. A research group at the Rand Corporation in Santa Monica has programmed a computer so that it even corrects human errors. Rand's Johnniac, named after the late Princeton mathematician John von Neumann, at ten years old, was eligible for retirement. But armed with instructions devised by expert programmer J. Clifford Shaw, it performed some impressive feats.

In one such demonstration, Shaw pushed the IN button and Johnniac started off by printing "Please type your initials." After Shaw complied, the following exchange took place:

SHAW: Type 1/0 [Instruction shorthand for "What is one divided by zero?"]

JOHNNIAC: Error in line above: malformed? [All instructions must end with a period.]

SHAW: TYPE 1/0.

JOHNNIAC: Error in line above: attempting division by zero.*

SHAW: Type sqrt (—3). [Shorthand for "What is the square root of minus 3?"]

JOHNNIAC: Error in line above: attempting sqrt of a negative number.

SHAW: Type sqrt (3).

JOHNNIAC: Sqrt (3) = +1.73205081.

* In 1946, Eniac, the first of the electronic computers, blew out several hundred of its vacuum tubes during a futile effort to divide by zero, because nobody remembered to program it with the information that the task is impossible.

This is a highly simplified illustration of Johnniac's capabilities. Similar question-answer procedures have been used in predicting satellite orbits, allocating weight distributions in space vehicles, and designing improved electronic circuits. One great value of on-the-spot debugging is that it teaches the investigator to be more accurate by the very process of pointing out mistakes immediately after they are made. According to one estimate, this feature could reduce the project time required to develop programs by more than 75 per cent.

MMMCLXXIII DIVIDED BY XLIX

Another problem of immediate concern to computer users is the development of new languages that permit them to communicate more easily with their electronic collaborators. Once investigators had to speak the machine's language, writing out long lists of instructions such as "120785501101" ("add 10 to the number at memory location 07855") and "390792-500100" ("type out the information in memory location 07925"). Ever since then the trend has mercifully been toward less awkward communication. Now computers can digest hybrids of plain English and number symbols. But even more natural languages are on the way.

One of the most effective and important new languages, known as STRESS (Structural Engineering System Solver), is being developed by Steven Fenves of the University of Illinois. It was invented in 1962 to promote engineer-computer communications in designing factories and other structures. STRESS has a vocabulary of about a hundred words that engineers customarily use in discussing problems among themselves and that they can now use to address a computer.

For example, after furnishing the machine with full information about the geometry of a building and the loads on its parts, an engineer may simply type "PRINT MEMBER FORCES" (that is, the forces acting on the joints of all supporting girders). To express the same idea using the number language of the old days would have meant writing out several hundred individual instructions, each consisting of twelve digits. Another command, "SOLVE," replaces more than 30,000 of the old numbered instructions. While about five weeks were required to achieve command of number languages, STRESS can be mastered in a few hours.

Fenves has used STRESS to analyze the effect of winds, weights of heavy machinery, and other forces on the structural-steel members of a proposed midwestern industrial plant. It was the sort of problem that would not even have been attempted by engineers using conventional computing techniques. Since a complete analysis would probably take a man a month of solid work, present custom is to settle for rather less information—which might be obtained in three or four days. Fenves required some two or three hours to prepare a suitable program, and the machine came up with a solution in exactly eighteen seconds. The enormous gain, of course, comes directly from using a language that promotes rather than impedes thinking. It is the difference between dividing 3173 by 49 and dividing MMMCLXXIII by XLIX—a difference which explains why many problems that high-school students solve routinely today were beyond the powers of ancient Rome's most talented mathematicians.

STRESS is only the beginning. The drive is toward more and more natural language. Conversations between man and machine will always be somewhat stilted until we have a computer that can understand idioms and interpret the particular meaning of a word or a sentence with several possible meanings. This is still a long way off, but a program written by Anthony Oettinger and Susumu Kuno of Harvard's Computation Laboratory permits a computer to list all possible meanings. "Time flies like an arrow" may seem fairly straightforward to us, but a machine sees a number of other possibilities—for example, "Time the speed of flies as quickly as you can" ("time" being interpreted as a verb rather than a noun) and "Certain flies enjoy an arrow" ("time" being interpreted as an adjective, and "like" being interpreted as a verb). The machine could be instructed to rule out these particular offbeat parsings, but how would it handle the sentence, "Fruit flies like bananas"? Problems of semantics continue to plague investigators concerned with advanced man-machine communication.

A COMPUTER THAT SAYS "HELLO"

Meanwhile work continues on improving hardware as well as software, and some fairly advanced gadgets are scheduled to make their appearance in a few years. Teletypewriters turn out to be quite useful for relaying messages to machines, but keyboards may soon be supplemented by new kinds of input devices. Herbert Teager, one of the most imaginative of M.I.T.'s practical-minded engineers, has invented a device that enables the computer user to communicate via messages written on paper rather than on a screen as in Sketchpad. Versions have been built at Rand Corporation and Brookhaven National Laboratory. The input table consists of a glass or plastic plate about the size of a window pane with a fine grid of electric wires in it. To communicate with a computer you simply put a piece of paper on top of the plate and write on it with a pen that is sensitive to the electric charge on the grid. As the pen is moved, information about its position is transmitted to the computer.

This system can be programmed to learn the style of each investigator working with it. It can recognize the way he writes any of several hundred characters, such as the letters of the alphabet, mathematical symbols, symbols representing transistors and other circuit elements, and so on. Then it is ready for action, say, as an aid in designing the acoustics of an auditorium. First the engineer draws a rough picture of the auditorium, writing appropriate instructions and equations on the same piece of paper. Then he asks the machine to figure out the room's acoustic characteristics. It may respond by drawing graphs, charts, and perhaps a revised picture indicating the shape of an auditorium with improved acoustics. A larger input table or "blackboard" is being built for experimental classroom use.

Direct voice communication may also come, although regular conversations cannot be expected in any hurry. For one thing, no one has yet come up with a recognition device that would permit an investigator to talk with computers the way he does with human colleagues. But "signing in" vocally has been done experimentally. Every voice has its unique sound patterns, and a machine can be taught to recognize a particular investigator's voice, and automatically prepare for his instructions. It may someday even greet him with a vibrant electronic "Hello."

One hardware requirement that will be vital in the very near future is much bigger memories. In present-day machines, data needed for high-speed calculations are stored in fast built-in memories from which any item of information can be retrieved in a millionth of a second or so. Most fast computer memories are made up of magnetic cores, doughnut-shaped elements about the size of pinheads, each representing a unit of information known as a "bit." A large computer may have a capacity of one million to four million bits, about equal to the information contained in a short book. (Eniac, the ancestor of all electronic computers, had a peanut-brain capacity of only two lines.)

But this is hardly enough for the coming breed of increasingly sophisticated computers. In the first place, extra storage space will be needed to hold the programs of instructions needed to make the machines extra intelligent. Besides, more and more basic information has to be crammed into the memory as investigators cope with more and more complicated problems. So the fast-access memories of the future will have 50 million to 100 million bits. The cost of a bit is expected to tumble from a current 25 to 30 cents to ½ cent or less, and the already minute memory cores will probably be replaced by even tinier spots of magnetic material deposited on thin glass films.

There is also likely to be a sharp increase in the capacity of slower-access external memories, corresponding roughly to reference libraries; these contain tables, programs, and data that can be used when needed but are not filed in high-speed memory. Currently, a large external memory may contain 100 million bits or more, stored on magnetic tapes or on special devices consisting of metal disks, from which information can be extracted through pickup units like the playing arms of jukeboxes. A short-term objective is to increase this sort of memory to about a trillion bits, enough information to fill a thousand sets of the *Encyclopaedia Britannica.* Some investigators are already looking beyond that to capacities 10,000 times greater, holding more information than is contained in all the world's libraries.

SIMULTANEOUS SERVICE FOR FORTY CUSTOMERS

The design of more resourceful computers is not enough by itself. We must learn to use them efficiently. Having a multimillion-dollar machine all to yourself for extended periods, as a kind of personal consultant, may be extremely helpful if you are an investigator doing creative work. But it makes no sense at all economically, and man-machine cooperation must be put on an economically sound basis.

Furthermore, a spectacular mismatch exists between human and computer speeds. Suppose it takes a minute to conceive a question and convey it to a machine. That is fast thinking by our standards, but it happens to be unbearably sluggish so far as the computer is concerned. During that minute of idle waiting it could have been churning out as many calculations as a human being could produce in a year of eight-hour working days. A decade is likely to be squandered every time an investigator stops for a coffee break, a century or more when he sits back to mull over a new idea.

Fortunately, there is a way of maintaining closer relations with a computer and also using it more efficiently. If the machines are too swift to be wasted on one man alone, let them serve a large number of people at once. This approach, known as time sharing, is already being tried at a number of research centers, notably including System Development Corporation in Santa Monica.

In a special "central processor area," System Development has installed a ninety-ton computer, I.B.M.'s $7-million Q32 (short for AN/FSQ-32V), which is a streamlined version of a computer built originally for the nation's radar-defense network. Forty investigators or research teams have access to the Q32 by remote control, through communication lines hooked to the computer from their own laboratories, which are fitted with teletypewriters and other equipment. The forty laboratories are like subscribers to a central telephone exchange. They get service merely by "dialing" the computer, which switches automatically from station to station and devotes a period or "quantum" of lightning-fast calculating time to each investigator in turn.

This idea is fairly simple, but working it out calls for some fancy traffic control. As a hypothetical example, suppose twenty users go "on the air" at once. The Q32 turns its attention to user No. 1, transferring his program from an external and relatively slow memory unit, a kind of circulating library, to its fast, built-in working memory in about a fortieth of a second. The machine devotes another fortieth of a second to the problem—the quantum, which on the Q32 represents about a month of human computing time—and still another fortieth of a second is consumed in shifting user No. 1's program back to external memory and bringing in user No. 2's program.

JUST LIKE THE MOVIES

On this schedule the machine takes a twentieth of a second to serve each user (about the time required for the wink of an eye), or a total of one second for all twenty users. Then it goes back to user No. 1 and repeats the cycle until the problems are solved. Actually, the workings of the time-sharing system are more complicated than this example indicates, but the general principle is that the machine is working at peak efficiency on a merry-go-round basis. It can be compared to a chess master playing many amateurs at once; he stops for a shrewd look at each board in turn, sizes up the situation swiftly, makes a strategic responding move, and then passes on to the next board.

Although the Q32's time is being shared, each user feels he is getting its full attention. The machine comes around to him every second or so, and it may take ten or more passes to handle his problem. But typing his instructions and the machine's responses take appreciably longer than that, so the user often begins receiving an answer as soon as he finishes asking his question. Since the machine's "reflexes" are so much faster than his, he has the illusion of continuity, the same sort of phenomenon that produces the illusion of motion at the movies.

A high degree of precision is essential to control such a system. All the information used by each time-sharing investigator, all his special data and instructions, must be shuttled back and forth between internal and external memories rapidly and as a single block or package. Furthermore, all the packages must be tightly sealed—that is, information must not be allowed to leak from one to another as sometimes happens during a long-distance telephone call when a conversation on another line interferes with your own conversation.

Comparable slip-ups during time sharing would be catastrophic. Information required for analyzing stock-market trends or the success of a simulated air attack might "leak" and interfere with the solution of a problem in nuclear physics, with results confusing to all parties concerned. Five computer experts at an east-coast research center once spent more than two days trying to spot the cause of an analogous leak, which involved a minor flaw in one electronic component. The best insurance against chaos in time sharing is a cleanly designed machine without unnecessarily complicated circuitry—plus an efficient "supervisor" or master program of instructions to synchronize the flow of microsecond events.

A great advantage of time-sharing systems is that the users need not be stationed in the same building that houses the computer. The machine at Carnegie Tech's computer center, for example, is connected by telephone lines to a station at a nuclear-research laboratory fifty miles away. Another line connects the machine with a teletypewriter in the home of Allen Newell, an investigator who is concerned with advanced programming and likes to work late into the night. Other "telephone booth" stations are located at undergraduate and graduate dormitories for students who may want practice in communicating with computers or high-grade help with their homework.

Special connections link System Development's computer to a computer at Stanford Research Institute at Palo Alto, and to laboratories at U.C.L.A., the University of California at Berkeley, and the Los Angeles Police Department. Recently M.I.T. experimented with transatlantic links to computing laboratories in Great Britain and Norway. It may not be long before other such networks are used experimentally for a variety of special purposes—three-way conversations involving a computer and two scientists working, perhaps in different nations, on different aspects of the same problem; exchanging new theories and discoveries by transmitting information directly from research laboratories to computer memories throughout the world; "hot line" computer-aided discussions among scientific, military, and political leaders.

THE VERSATILITY OF MAC

In 1963, M.I.T. played host to more than a hundred investigators from university and government laboratories throughout the nation, as well as representatives of half a dozen computer manufacturers. They came to discuss all aspects of basic computer science—and to help shape the plans of an organization formed recently to speed the development of new computer systems. The organization is known as Project MAC, an acronym standing for two things: (1) Machine-Aided Cognition, and (2) Multiple-Access Computer, or time sharing. The Advanced Research Projects Agency is providing funds.

MAC has its own large central computer connected with twenty-four communicating stations, and twenty-six more stations are expected to be operating soon. Its research staff, consisting of M.I.T. investigators and colleagues invited from other centers, are conducting a variety of studies. On the business side, for example, a computer program simulates work at Westinghouse's steam-turbine plant in South Philadelphia, the aim being to use up-to-the-minute records of current operations in improving production schedules. Another project is a system for providing at a moment's notice similar records of bills paid and funds committed in the running of MAC itself. Experience gained along these lines is sure to be applied to larger-scale problems, such as introducing advanced automation into the New York Stock Exchange, as recommended in an SEC staff study. (Stock Exchange automation may also be investigated on the time-sharing system at Carnegie Tech.)

Engineers are working on methods of storing in a computer's memory information about hundreds of thousands of standard parts. With such a setup, a designer could state that his job requires, say, a square-headed bolt a quarter of an inch in diameter and four inches long with twenty-six threads to the inch—and receive the following answer: "There are no such bolts with twenty-six threads to the inch. We have twenty or eighteen threads; which do you want?" The MAC computer is also being used to study automatic language translation, information retrieval, a three-dimensional version of Sketchpad, and improved highway designs.

Investigators concerned with these and other developments are playing a double role. They are working on their own problems, of course. But at the same time they are contributing to the solution of a much broader problem that in a sense is a composite of all their individual problems. Time sharing, as a practical way of giving many investigators a chance to communicate directly with large-scale computers, is a deliberate effort to increase the power of the human mind, to amplify intelligence. Project MAC has sociological as well as technological overtones. "Here at M.I.T. we have a sample community of very bright and highly motivated people," explains Robert Fano, professor of electrical engineering and MAC director. "We are working primarily with them and for them. Our task is to discover new ways of using computers to help them in creative activity."

A MECHANICAL I.Q. BOOSTER

The next generation of computers is coming soon. Project MAC investigators see the need in a few years for a prototype computer far more advanced than any existing now. It will have an internal memory of more than a million words, operate at least ten times faster than current models (performing a decade's worth of human calculations in a minute), and share its time with some 250 users. Development costs are estimated at about $20 million. Computer manufacturers, of course, have shown intense interest in these plans.

Such machines will offer mankind something as significant and perhaps as frightening as the energy of the nucleus itself, a practically unlimited supply of thinking power. A new public utility is in the making, an information utility that will make logic available at established rates to subscribers throughout the world—technicians controlling national air-traffic and defense systems, executives at board-of-directors meetings demonstrating the effects of controversial sales or advertising policies, housewives seeking best buys from a master shopping catalogue, engineers consulting invisible electronic draftsmen to help them design a new satellite (or a new computer).

The information utility may well have its most dramatic impact on education. This is where you begin to sense the start of a spiraling process, a kind of intellectual Operation Bootstrap. It is not only a matter of time-shared computers carrying on conversations with hundreds or thousands of pupils at once, although that is certainly on the way. As the success of Sketchpad and other projects indicates, a student at a computer can do a great deal more than a student alone. In effect his I.Q. is raised by a measurable amount. (A fairly bright and properly trained fourteen-year-old should have no trouble doubling or tripling his score with the benefit of an electronic alter ego.)

Some time ago Charles Miller, head of M.I.T.'s Department of Civil Engineering, assigned a problem to his freshman class: the design of one ramp of a highway clover-leaf intersection. Using a computer and a special language that Miller developed recently, the students had no trouble at all with the problem. They solved it in about twenty minutes including a few seconds of machine time, and one student voiced the general complaint that it was much too easy. The significant thing about this story is that the problem was a formidable senior-level task and had never before been given to freshmen.

So, at least as far as such work is concerned, a freshman plus a computer is smarter than a computerless senior—probably several orders of magnitude smarter. The following year Miller's freshmen were asked to design the entire clover leaf. When logic can be tapped as readily as electricity, similar results may be expected at all levels from grade to graduate school and beyond. This is intelligence amplification with a vengeance. Man appears finally to be on the verge of using the full powers of his mind.

4

The "Assault" on Fortress I.B.M.

NOTHING AROUSES more amusement in computer circles than the title of this chapter. "Fortress is the word for I.B.M. all right," comments one specialist wryly. "But who is going to assault it and when?" A fair question indeed. Almost before the business world had a chance to size up what was going on, I.B.M. consolidated its dominant position in the young and booming computer industry, which it formally entered in 1953, and moved into a position of competitive strength probably unparalleled in business history.

For a while, back in 1962, it looked as if the "assault on fortress I.B.M." (as it was actually described) *was* gathering way. I.B.M.'s seven major competitors, taking them together, seemed finally to have mustered enough strength and wisdom to reduce the giant to size. Solemn and plausible predictions were made to the effect that I.B.M., like General Motors, would presently be forced to settle for less than 60 per cent of the market. Such speculation, late figures reveal, was premature, to say the least. Partly because more than three-quarters of all computers are leased and not sold outright, computer makers do not release figures on the dollar volume of the hardware they ship in any given year. But specialists have compiled roughly accurate estimates of each company's hardware in use, and the likeliest of these estimates are embodied in the chart on page 76. In January, 1961, the chart suggests, I.B.M. accounted for 71 per cent of the $1.8 billion worth of general-purpose computers then in use. But at the start of 1964, when I.B.M. was expected to be quaking under its assailants' blows, it accounted for about 76 per cent of the $5.3 billion worth of machines then in use. Between January, 1961, and the end of 1963, in other words, I.B.M. seems to have done a lot better than its competitors taken together. Although the estimates are very rough, they surely justify the observation that I.B.M. was far from being hurt or even menaced. And although some competitors increased their share of the "market" more than I.B.M., their prospects do not justify the prediction that any of them will menace fortress I.B.M. very much or very soon.

One reason is that on April 7, 1964, in what Chairman Thomas J. Watson, Jr., called the most important product announcement in the company's history, I.B.M. introduced a whole new "family" of computers. This new line, called System/360 presumably because it will encompass all 360 degrees of the computer world, embodies many technical advances, such as microminiature circuits and greatly improved accessory devices; and it will both lower I.B.M.'s manufacturing costs and increase enormously the machines' speed and "computation per dollar" of cost to user. Never regarded as a pacesetter in computer hardware, I.B.M. finally has a first-rate line of "compatible" machines—i.e., they use the same language, and hence can be instructed or programmed alike. System/360 will eventually replace the whole present I.B.M. line, which contains many weak spots that its rivals have deftly exploited, and will more than compete head on with existing machines. As one competitor exclaimed, more in sorrow than in contempt, "And now I.B.M. is selling real computers—alas!" The new series, as we shall see, may have its troubles. But by midsummer 1964 customers had spoken for more than $1.2 billion worth of System/360 equipment. Although many orders may be no more than priority reservations, I.B.M.'s new line appears a thumping success.

Before the fanfare had died away, computer experts were reviving earlier prophecies that the ranks of the computer-hardware manufacturers would eventually be thinned down considerably. I.B.M.'s seven major rivals are Sperry Rand, R.C.A., Control Data, G.E., N.C.R., Burroughs, and Honeywell; and among the dozen or so minor ones are specialists like Bunker-Ramo, General Precision, Scientific Data Systems, Advanced Scientific Instruments, and Digital Equipment Corporation. Some prophets, among them the redoubtable William Norris, founder and president of Control Data Corporation, the most successful of the seven, predicted that the seven majors will be reduced to five. And even Norris avoids the question of how much of the market the five surviving companies will enjoy.

The rest of the industry reacted to the new series with studied undismay, and this stance was not wholly put on. Every computer company makes or can readily buy some components more advanced than those in System/360, and most companies are announcing "revolutionary" new models of their own. The big question, however, is not so much whether they can produce better hardware soon enough, but what all this competition will do to their earning power, and

Value of General-Purpose Computers in Operation

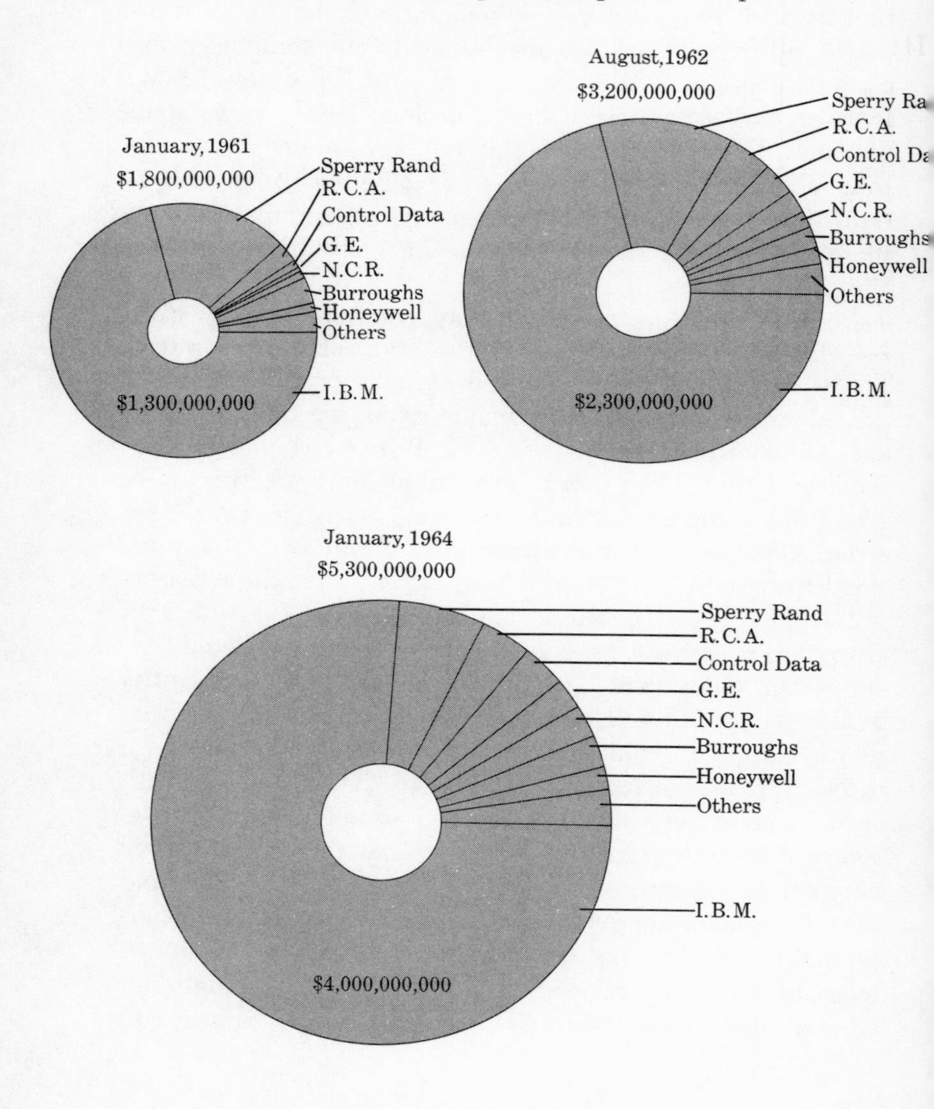

III. THE BIGGER THE PIE, THE BIGGER THE BITE FOR I.B.M.

For a long time experts plausibly argued that I.B.M. would lose ground to hard-hitting competitors. But the charts on the facing page, which show the dollar value of computer hardware (including "peripheral" equipment) operating in the United States, tell a different story. The data for the charts, admittedly rough, was compiled by Frederic Withington of Arthur D. Little, Inc., from many informed estimates, and excludes special military and space computers, punched-card tabulators, and accounting machines. In January, 1961, I.B.M. accounted for 71 per cent or $1,285 million of computer hardware then in use; in August, 1962, it still accounted for 71 per cent or $2,260 million. But by January 1, 1964, it accounted for 76 per cent or $4,060 million of the hardware in use. If these estimates are even approximately right, I.B.M. actually increased its share. Over the three-year period, it is true, nearly all except Sperry Rand increased their share of the "market" more than I.B.M.; in a sense, I.B.M. held its position at the expense of Sperry Rand. But most of them started from a very low figure in 1961, which made it easy to show a large percentage increase. And between August 1962 and January 1964 most of them did not do as well as I.B.M.

Although the cumulative value of all hardware in use will continue to increase steeply, the *annual* value of hardware shipments may level off somewhat until late in 1965, when I.B.M. begins to deliver its new line. In both 1963 and 1964 total value of hardware shipments was around $1.7 billion. Outlays for software or programming and other services, most of which went to computer manufacturers, came to more than $1.2 billion. In addition, the industry turned out special-order military and space computers worth more than $1.2 billion, and the analog-computermakers took in another $45 million or more.

whether they can beat I.B.M. at the game of persuading customers to buy the machines. Of the seven, only Control Data has been turning a profit on computers, and that partly because it has been selling most of its production outright. Taken together, they have probably invested close to $1 billion in computers and the "peripheral" hardware and services that go with them. Now, thanks to I.B.M.'s System/360, the "sales life" of most machines is bound to be shortened, and long-term development and production costs for most, if not all, companies seem bound to rise. Their profitability, so long postponed, may well be postponed further.

THE PLUSH-LINED RAT RACE

From the start, electronic data processing, considering the investment required, attracted a surprising number of companies. Some office-machine firms had no choice; they either had to get into computers or out of office machines. But many saw an opportunity without parallel. The computer, as previous chapters have explained, is expanding human productivity to new levels by expanding human brainpower to hitherto superhuman levels. The computer industry, therefore, is probably growing faster than any other capital-goods industry on record, and making computers and their equipment seems the most potentially rewarding of all capital-goods activities. The risks of the game, looked at with the optimism and acumen of any good entrepreneur, seem to fade into insignificance compared to the potential rewards.

Suppose you are a computer maker with a line of machines you have modestly called the Superdoop, and that your Superdoop II is a hot model. Lease enough numbers of Superdoop II long enough, and you are in the dough. The fact that your tooling-up expenses—and your immediate losses—are very heavy only exhilarates you; as you tell your friends, if you make money too early in this game you know you are not a success. By the fourth year after you install a model, you may have your money back and the gravy will roll in. If your customers use your machines more than eight hours a day, moreover, the gravy will flow sooner, for rentals customarily rise 40 per cent for each extra shift the machine is used. By, say, the sixth year after you have begun work on a model, you may have recovered your costs and your profits will pile up at the rate of 30 per cent or so a year on your now amortized investment. Even if the annual value of your shipments does not increase for a few years, your net income will go right on rising elegantly because rentals increase as you install new models. And the fluctuations of the marketplace will harass you little. Your installations may drop 25 per cent in a given year, but your billings, because they consist overwhelmingly of rentals, will hardly show it. That is the way I.B.M. grew great, you say, and that is the way you can grow great.

Alas, it does not necessarily work that way. When competition is intense, the apparent advantages of the system can turn into disadvantages, and all the rewards can keep on receding into the future. From the time a model is conceived to the time it is scrapped, you have already discovered, the electronic computer is the most demanding machine ever created. You need technical geniuses and superlative managerial judgment and vision, and you need enough money for them to operate without inhibition—money for years of research and development, for staggeringly expensive components and plant, for $25,000-a-year salesmen and engineering talent to back them up, for $18,000-a-year programmers and other "software" specialists in the art of preparing data for the machine, and for service men who may make even more than plumbers and electricians. Two or three years of toil may go into developing a model, and a year or more into producing it, often followed by a year or so of sweating it out with the customer while the machine is being "debugged" and otherwise brought on line.

Now let us indulge in a little more fiction based on reality and suppose that any one of several competitive situations overtakes your marketing strategy for Superdoop II. Suppose, first, that it is only moderately well received, either because you miscalculated its merits or because a competitor charged in early with a "sensational" model. Your production costs, because you make fewer models than you had hoped, will be a little less than you had planned, but your development costs are history, and you end up with little if any profit. And if the competitive model is very hot, you may have to take back some of your older machines before they have made money. These you will have to scrap or sell at a steep discount.

Or suppose your Superdoop II does turn out to be a hot number. Either because you have had technical trouble or because you waited to see what another competitor was going to do, however, this great model is a year or so "late." You tool up for a big volume and rub your hands as you think ahead to the day when rentals start coming in. But your tardiness has lost a year of rentals; and your blasted competitor comes up with a better model not long after you have sunk a lot of money into plant and equipment. Despite your big temporary success, your development plus manufacturing costs again leave you with very little return, even over the long run. Your only course may be a crash program for your Superdoop III, which you had planned to bring out later on. So you end up "obsoleting" your own as well as your competitor's machines, and your profits again recede.

In all these circumstances, of course, you can cut prices, just as practically everybody does. But you do not need a Ph.D. to tell you that too much price cutting can rob you of resources to carry on your development and marketing, and that without these you cannot produce or sell as you must tomorrow. Selling machines outright instead of leasing them can also help you out of tight spots. Fortunately for many companies, the federal government, the largest single computer customer, is trying to induce its agencies to buy more machines, and more non-government sales may be made outright. But in the long run, lease or sell, the problem is much the same. Unless you can count on an average life of about five years, you are in a plush-lined rat race, with the tantalizing goal more often than not eluding your grasp.

EDUCATE TO SELL

And why do not I.B.M.'s goals elude its grasp? Sometimes they do; like everybody else, I.B.M. has made mistakes, and it has not been inordinately favored by the gods. However, it did enter the electronic-data-processing field with one big advantage. Long before the possibilities of EDP were understood, I.B.M. was an immensely prosperous company that had captured the bulk of the world's "unit record" or punched-card tabulating-machine business. Since most data is fed into computers by punched cards, this gave the company a prime market for computers. It also provided a magnificent profit base. I.B.M. now owns about $2 billion worth of punched-card machines, which in 1963 probably fetched it at least $500 million in rentals and may have accounted for nearly half its pretax net of $589 million. Owing in good part to this lucrative activity, nearly a third of the company's total assets ($2.4 billion) are in the form of cash or its equivalent. As one competitor quips, what makes I.B.M. such a fortress is cash, resources, cash, liquid assets, earnings, and cash.

But the mere possession of ample means is no guarantee that they will be risked at all, to say nothing of being risked intelligently. The distinguishing characteristic of I.B.M. is that it is bursting with resourcefulness as well as resources, and that once it decides to commit both to a project, it commits without stint. Having built several experimental electronic vacuum-tube computers back in the early 1950s, I.B.M. thought it had good reasons for not manufacturing them. As a matter of fact, founder Thomas J. Watson turned down the chance to buy Eckert-Mauchly, the pioneer company in the field. Just how and why he changed his mind is an involved tale half lost in the twilight of corporate legend; but about 1953, having grasped the promises of electronic computers, I.B.M. charged into the field with characteristic energy.

As the purchaser of Eckert-Mauchly, Remington Rand (now Sperry Rand) had a long headstart. But by early 1956, I.B.M. was out in front. What put it far ahead was the same kind of aggressive salesmanship that had made it supreme in the tabulating-machine field. I.B.M. saw at once that the computer, because nearly everybody was so densely ignorant of its potentialities, needed to be sold in a more creative way than even the tabulating machine. While Remington Rand limped along, paying more attention to technical matters than to selling, I.B.M. aggressively educated prospects on what computers could do for them, and how to use them.

I.B.M. has emphatically not neglected technical matters; it now spends more than $125 million annually on research and development, or more than the billings of many of its competitors. Its Thomas J. Watson Research Center, although dating back only to 1961, has already acquired a formidable reputation. But it is the money that I.B.M. spends on sales and service that makes it unique. From laboratory to controller, from shop to executive suite, the company is primarily one big mechanism for pushing machines into the market and making them work. On everything that comes under the heading of selling, I.B.M. spends nearly $400 million a year, or nearly 20 per cent of its revenues. Its Data Processing Division, which sells, installs, and services the machines, employs about 32,000 people, including a force of more than 8,500 well-trained salesmen and sales engineers. A large percentage of salesmen boast advanced degrees, and many specialize in specific industries, about which they are remarkably well informed; the only thing they have in common with the old-time I.B.M. salesman with his "sincere" suit, white shirt, and protruding shirt cuffs, is superb discipline and the cocksureness that goes with representing what they are convinced is the best outfit in the world. The pressure to produce is not perhaps quite so heavy and obvious as it was in the old days when, some say, a man who lost the order lost his job; but the pressure is still there.

No group of salesmen is reinforced more deeply with special insight and talent. When a salesman visits a likely prospect, he may take along a systems engineer, and the two together may spend days or weeks on end showing the prospect how a computer can save money and solve problems. After the prospect is formally converted into a customer, the real selling begins. Maintaining the world's largest stock of ready-made programs and nearly 3,000 programmers, I.B.M. helps the company train people to use the computer, and usually invites them to spend two weeks at one of its classes scattered around in 159 U.S. cities. The company's education department, set up by Thomas J. Watson in 1916, spends upwards of $60 million a year instructing 150,000 employees and customers in free courses that cover everything from maintenance and programming to the history and concept of the computer. What is more, educating the customer's technicians does not end the process of dispensing enlightenment about computers. The salesman and systems engineer show the customer how the machine can solve more problems than he ever dreamed it could, and presently I.B.M. may invite a top executive or two to attend a seminar on his industry's problems, or a general course in computer concepts. "We don't sell a product," says Frank Cary, an I.B.M. data-processing vice-president; "we sell solutions to problems." Which is why I.B.M. ends up selling so many products.

THE BIG UMBRELLA

Because I.B.M.'s services are so copiously available and its image so favorably recognized, it can keep its prices high enough to support its multifarious services and turn a handsome profit in the bargain. Generally, it assumes a lordly indifference to competitors' "special arrangements," i.e., price cutting. Not long ago, one story has it, an I.B.M. salesman was informed that his rival proposed to install a comparable system for 25 per cent less than I.B.M.'s price; the salesman loftily commented that the rival should have offered 35 per cent off. This is not to say that I.B.M. never cuts prices; it customarily makes handsome special concessons to "prestige" customers like institutions, and occasionally slugs it out for other strategic orders. But I.B.M.'s price level is "set," and the fact seems to be that if it really made a policy of cutting prices, it could drive many if not most of its competitors out of business. What doubtless stays its hand is not so much the threat of antitrust as simple economics: price reductions would probably lose more profit than the additional business would gain. Some competitors are openly grateful. "I.B.M.'s price umbrella is our biggest asset," says one. "If we could only show it on our balance sheet!"

Far from resting on its puissance, I.B.M. behaves as if the wolves were howling outside the door. "When I read the papers about how our competitors are predicting what they will do," says Chairman Watson, "I clip them and paste them on my mirror."

Actually, I.B.M.'s biggest problems are internal. One is how to bring up enough talent in the company to take over new responsibilities, and another is what to do with all its cash. Probably the most bothersome problem goes under the somewhat euphemistic label of "impact prediction," or how to advance the ball without fumbling it. Since the vast bulk of I.B.M. machines are owned by I.B.M., every new model must be created for its effect not merely on competitors' machines but on the company's own; in fact, I.B.M. probably worries much more about its own innovations than its competitors'. It would achieve a hollow victory if its customers enthusiastically signed up for new I.B.M. models and sent back all their old ones before they had earned their keep. This is one reason I.B.M. has not exactly been a pioneer in hardware techniques, and why its decision to build a completely new line came hard. It could have brought out a few new machines in the large and very small sizes, where its products are weakest, and gone on enjoying its dominance for some time. But it would have had a technically obsolescent line, increasingly vulnerable to competitors with better equipment.

As all alert enterprisers are well aware, the time for a competitive business to change is just when everything is going better than it has ever gone before. So I.B.M. designed a whole new family consisting of six central processors and nineteen variations, all compatible or amenable to programming in the same "language," and equally suited for scientific and business use. System/360 features capacious memories, forty-four kinds of improved peripheral equipment, and tiny microelectronic circuits that give the machines up to five times the speed of their predecessors. If I.B.M. were designing the line today, it might use smaller and faster "integrated" circuits, but at the time it made the decision the most economic choice was the so-called ceramic microelectronic unit. However, System/360 is designed to accommodate integrated circuits, and at all events is expected to have a long operating life, so that a customer can both meet his growing needs and get the benefit of new techniques without going to the expense of reprogramming.

At first glance, I.B.M. might seem to have taken little calculated risk in making System/360. But the smaller machines in the new line will not be delivered until the autumn of 1965, and the larger ones not till well into 1966; this may give competitors time to make off with some business by leapfrogging I.B.M. with improved varieties of their own computers. Moreover, System/360 will be *in*compatible with nearly all I.B.M.'s present machines except the best-selling 1400 series, and not wholly compatible with them. This may mean that I.B.M. will have to take back many machines it now has out on lease, or that competitors' customers will avoid new programming expenses by going along with improved versions of competitors' models. And the compatibility of all machines in System/360 may tempt competitors to build improved imitations of System/360. "Don't bet we won't zero in on this target," says one. I.B.M.'s risks, however, seem more than offset by the potential gains, particularly as System/360 expands its acceptance.

THE ORDEALS OF UNIVAC

The least threatening of I.B.M.'s seven major rivals has been Sperry Rand's Univac Division, the successor to Remington Rand's computer activities. Few enterprises have ever turned out so excellent a product and managed it so ineptly. Univac came in too late with good models, and not at all with others; and its salesmanship and software were hardly to be mentioned in the same breath with I.B.M.'s. The upper ranks of other computer companies are studded with ex-Univac people who left in disillusionment. Although Univac still clings to second place, its share of the installed market declined from close to 100 per cent a dozen or so years ago to about 7 per cent in January, 1964. In the process it probably dropped more than $200 million.

To set things to rights, Sperry Rand somewhat belatedly (in May, 1962) brought in Dr. Louis T. Rader, an I.T.&T. executive with a reputation for getting things done. Dr. Rader laid about him with zeal, and by late 1963 had apparently reversed Univac's long decline. That year Univac, according to its own figures, increased its domestic installed dollar value of computer hardware by 23 per cent and of tabulating equipment by 35 per cent. To cure its software deficiencies, it retained Computer Sciences Corporation, which developed program systems for the 1107 and Univac III, its largest machines.

Although Univac's marketing organization was still regarded as weak, it landed the biggest computer order ever written, for an inventory-control system covering the Air Force's 152 bases throughout the world. (I.B.M., G.E., and R.C.A. also bid on the job.) The system will use 152 Univac 1050 Model II Real Time systems with appropriate peripheral equipment, and will fetch the company, over five years, a total of around $50 million, including purchase, rental, and maintenance. Univac's campaign was conducted by Lee Johnson, star salesman and head of the company's federal-government marketing division, with a large staff of technicians. At 2:00 P.M. November 4, 1963, eight months after the invitation to bid, Johnson received a call from the Air Force to stand by. "I couldn't be sure what it meant because I knew the Air Force would call winner and losers alike," he says. "Waiting was agony." After an hour of agony, the good word came.

Having done a lot of development for the military, including what it describes as the world's most advanced miniaturized computer, Sperry Rand does not lack the technical expertise for new models; and recently announced an advanced Univac 1108, five times as fast as its predecessor the 1107. But in July, 1964, the company's prospects took a turn for the worse when Dr. Rader, like so many Univac officials before him, abruptly resigned to join a competitor—in this instance, General Electric. And as this goes to press, Univac is still struggling to get itself in the black.

WHO IS IN THIRD PLACE?

Until recently third place in the computer business was generally accorded to R.C.A., whose net installations rose steeply from an estimated $45 million in January, 1961, to an estimated $190 million in January, 1964. But both backlog and installations may be vulnerable to the new I.B.M. line; R.C.A.'s big sellers, the 301 and 501, are regarded in the trade as outmoded by System/360. R.C.A. claims its new 3301, a fairly recent model, is the industry's strongest rival to System/360, because it is both available and "superior on a cost and performance basis." To push the 3301 along, it cut prices by as much as 40 per cent, and was duly rewarded with increased orders. R.C.A. claims to have gotten its computer business into the black, but it may be sacrificing the future for a good immediate showing. "Even General Sarnoff cannot have his share of the computer pie and eat it too," comments one specialist.

Edging into third place is the most aggressive and fastest growing of I.B.M.'s competitors, and the only sizable company aside from I.B.M. to profit consistently on computers: Control Data Corporation of Minneapolis. Founded in 1957 by William Norris, a laconic Nebraskan who learned about computers as vice-president of Univac, C.D.C. raised revenues from practically nothing in 1958 to around $121 million in the fiscal year ending in June, 1964, and showed a profit of some $6 million. Norris made money because he set new standards of costs and prices by selling (rather than leasing) his machines to sophisticated scientific users like research institutions, which do not need much service education or software. He also made money by watching costs closely and setting up a unique planning system that gives every employee an assigned role in the plan. His 6600 system, priced between $5 and $7 million, is the world's most powerful computer; so far he has sold three—one to the Atomic Energy Commission's Lawrence Radiation Laboratories, one to the National Center for Hemispheric Research, and one to CERN, the European organization for nuclear research.

It is Norris' aim to gain second place in computers by cultivating not only the scientific but the industrial process-control field, and he has accordingly broadened his line—and his expense base—considerably. He also leased more equipment, for which he had to provide software. Even before System/360 was announced, Norris found the going somewhat harder. Then came System/360. Trade gabble has it that the success of C.D.C.'s powerful computers, particularly the 6600 series, had injured I.B.M.'s prestige, and that System/360 was designed partly with C.D.C. in mind. Norris does not seem bothered, but stoutly avers that his computers still have a large price advantage, which is what counts with sophisticated customers; and he has announced new models at both the small and large end of his line. It will be late in 1965 before System/360 will be competing head on with C.D.C.; whether C.D.C. can then keep on taking business away from I.B.M. remains to be seen.

HONEYWELL'S "LIBERATOR"

Like C.D.C., Honeywell's data-processing division has done well against I.B.M. but, unlike C.D.C., which originally took the "rifle" approach to specific areas of the market, Honeywell aimed to meet I.B.M. across the board. Set up in 1955 under a shrewd Midwesterner named Walter Finke, the data-processing division had more than $100 million worth of machines operating in the commercial market early in 1964. It scored a *coup de maître* late in 1963 when it announced its 200 series, which is superior to and cheaper than I.B.M.'s hugely successful medium-sized 1400 series. With refreshing candor, Finke says Honeywell simply built a better version of the 1400 series. Not content with making it compatible with the I.B.M. line, he audaciously advertised it as the "liberator" because it would free owners of the 1400s from their limitations. "We figured I.B.M. was too smart not to let us take 10 per cent or so of the market," says Chuan Chu, an ex-Sperry Rand man who is now in charge of the company's EDP technical department. By March, 1964, it looked as if Finke had sized up things aright; backlog was greater than the total value of installations.

Shortly afterward, however, I.B.M. announced System/360. Although rumor had it that Honeywell's backlog was melting away, it seems to have held up well. According to a report by Frederic Withington of Arthur D. Little, Inc., the Honeywell 200 will have a $600-a-month advantage over the new I.B.M. competitive model. As for the rest of Honeywell's line, the company has announced a new 300 aimed at the scientific market, and has followed it with a compatible and more powerful 2200.

Appropriately enough, National Cash Register, the company that taught no less a master than Thomas J. Watson how to sell, may have to worry less about I.B.M. than most other major competitors. The reason lies in the kind of business N.C.R. (as it now prefers to be known) does. The company is not primarily a computer manufacturer, but a producer of cash registers and accounting and bookkeeping machines whose utility is immensely enhanced by certain kinds of computers, which N.C.R. duly makes. N.C.R. also markets a wide variety of peripheral equipment and supports a network of data-processing centers that provide computer services to retailers and in effect to anybody who owns a cash register with a punched-tape recorder. N.C.R.'s computer business has been gratifyingly successful; net installations rose from an estimated $20 million in January, 1961, to an estimated $125 million three years later. Precisely because it has done so well, N.C.R., which has invested more than $100 million in computers, does not expect to make money on them until well into 1965. But N.C.R. finds little to cheer about in System/360. Although it has equipped its 315 with a capacious thin film main memory, it may have to improve the 315 further or replace it before the model has achieved the elegantly profitable sales life every computer maker dreams about.

Much the same goes for Burroughs, which has also spent more than $100 million on computers without yet making money on its investment. Its 200 series has been reasonably successful; its 5000, a large machine with many advanced and some third generation characteristics, was introduced only in 1963, and has probably not yet sold well enough to pay off. Unless it can beat System/360, it may never pay off; and unless it can be modified to use common "languages" it probably will have trouble with System/360.

In January, 1964, Burroughs' net installations (excluding accounting-type machines) were around $120 million. Burroughs is one of the bigger computer producers for the military, whose purchases from the company have been running around $100 million a year. This work has given it unusual abilities in advanced techniques, and it is now bringing out an improved 300 series. Although computer rental income is rising, development costs are rising, too, and Burroughs probably will not break even on computers until sometime in 1966.

OUT TO CHALLENGE I.B.M.

The biggest unknown quantity in the business is General Electric, which formally got into electronic data processing only in 1959, four years after it landed a $30-million job for the Bank of America. There are many good reasons why G.E. could bulk large in computers. It is the world's biggest commercial user of the machines, and has not only a large captive market but a vast experience with them. G.E. also has the resources, financial and technical, to make a go of computers.

About 1960, G.E. began to move. It announced that it

would compete on a wide front, with emphasis on process control, banking, and communications, and would soon challenge I.B.M. itself. Striving also to get into the railroad field, it landed a contract to install an on-line, real-time control system on the Western Pacific Railroad. It built up a sales force of 200, opened a new plant at Phoenix, and developed a line of peripheral machines, while net value of its installations soared from $5 million in early 1961 to about $125 million in January, 1964.

By the following summer it looked as if G.E. had decided to go places. It announced new high speed, compatible models. It hired Dr. Rader away from Sperry Rand. And in a series of sharp and lucky moves, it strengthened immeasurably its European position by acquiring no less than a 49 per cent interest in the overextended Compagnie des Machines Bull of France, second largest European computer maker (after I.B.M.). G.E. also bought an interest in Italy's Olivetti, which makes computers as well as other business machines.

ROUGH TIMES AHEAD

As a group, I.B.M.'s major competitors have certain forces working in their favor. Many are immensely resourceful, most are improving their marketing as well as their hardware, and all are determined. Since I.B.M. cannot do everything at once, they can theoretically match it by concentrating on special segments of the market. And since the market, taking one year with another, is increasing by about 20 per cent a year, a company does not have to increase its share at all to grow at an enviable rate. Some believe that U.S. industry, once the computer business settles down and becomes less various, will tend to buy as it always has bought capital goods—i.e., will go out of its way, everything else being equal, to preserve alternative sources of supply.

What competitors doubtless hope will help them is the threat of antitrust prosecution. In 1956, I.B.M. signed a consent decree agreeing to offer to sell as well as lease its punched-card tabulators and computers, to get rid of part of its punched-card business (80 or 90 per cent of the market), to make certain patents available to others, and to convert its Service Bureau Corporation, which does retail data processing, into a separate company.

Things being what they are, the Department of Justice does not lack for new complaints. Most agree that splitting up I.B.M., which is suggested from time to time, makes little sense, if only because most of its competitors are big and much less homogeneous than I.B.M. But some make the case that I.B.M. should price its hardware, services, and software separately. "I.B.M. can charge high prices because it gives so much service 'free' along with the machine," explains one observer. "It may sell a machine for, say, $2 million, make a profit of $1 million on the machine, spend $500,000 on hand holding, and charge only nominally for service. The competitor, because it cannot match I.B.M.'s manufacturing costs and charges a lower price to boot, may make only $200,000 on a similar machine, and has little left for hand holding." If every company charged separately for service, software, and hardware, in other words, competitors would have a better chance.

The flaw in the argument is that I.B.M. enjoys a huge superiority in hardware costs and probably a considerable one in other costs, and if it were forced to separate its functions it would be obliged to price all its products and services more competitively. In an industry that often gives silent thanks for I.B.M.'s umbrella, this would be little gain. Although software sales could easily be separated from hardware sales, it is hard to see how services, including education, could in practice be separated from the sales of computers themselves. A computer is not a stock item like a dynamo or a gearbox, and what the average customer needs, in the frustrating days when he is learning how to use his baffling new machine, are service men who know it as those who conceived it and built it know it. Even if a customer had to pay separately for hardware, education, and services, he might be disposed to let I.B.M. tender him the bills.

Considering everything in their favor, I.B.M.'s competitors may on balance continue to hurt one another more than I.B.M. Granted that capital-goods buyers customarily prefer alternative suppliers, the run of computer buyers still likes to play safe with so huge, complex, and demanding an investment. Granted that competitors will equal or surpass I.B.M.'s hardware—which may be an unwarranted assumption in view of I.B.M.'s huge and growing competence in R. and D.—they may find it tougher than ever to approach I.B.M.'s manufacturing costs. Above all, they face the quality and force of I.B.M.'s marketing, which in the past has more than overcome any shortcomings, real or fancied, in I.B.M. hardware. "I.B.M. sells so well that it can sell dogs like hot cakes," remarks one software man, "and it isn't selling dogs." The history of U.S. business contains many examples of ferociously determined companies that have made headway against what seemed like almost insuperable competition. But few if any industries have thrown up a company so formidably powerful in everything that counts as I.B.M., and it is only noting the obvious to suggest that its rivals face harder going than they've experienced so far.

NO BOILING OIL ON THESE BOYS

Not everybody in the computer industry is locked in mortal struggle with I.B.M. "While the big boys who are trying to scale fortress I.B.M. are getting boiling oil poured on them," says one enterpriser jubilantly, "we are quietly going in the side door and making off with our share of the treasure." By "we" he meant the leasing companies. They operate on the premise that a computer at the right price has a longer economic life than is assumed in the manufacturer's rentals, which recover the list price of the machine in forty-five to fifty months. The leasing companies buy the used machines at a discount and rent them to customers at reduced rates. Largest in the field seems to be Boothe Leasing Corporation, a subsidiary of Greyhound Corporation, whose most popular plan provides a minimum saving of 10 per cent. Boothe does not plan to recover its investment from its first customer with such a deal, but expects ultimately to find another home for the machine; and it offers various schemes that encourage the renter to use the computer intensively. The rate for the first three years, for example, may provide little savings if the machine is used only one shift during the day. But it is cheaper than the manufacturers' rates for two shifts, still cheaper for three shifts. In any event, after the third year the rent goes down steeply. Such plans, if popular, could upset the industry's current price structure, which compels a company to pay just as much rent for a six-year-old machine as for the same model brand-new.

It is the theory of John Randolph, vice-president of Boothe Leasing, that computers should rent at rates (or sell at prices) that reflect their obsolescence, and that this practice would greatly extend the economic life of the machines.

Just as the steadily declining price of used cars has expanded the car market, he argues, so a steadily declining rental or price structure would expand the computer market. To help buyers of used computers employ them profitably, Boothe has even set up a software department. Although computer makers, too, can cut rentals and prices of older machines, Boothe is going ahead on the proposition that there will always be room for smart operators under the industry's "big umbrella."

Adventurous companies are expanding aggressively in other profitable fringes of the computer industry. There are, for example, the makers of peripheral and input-output devices such as tape scanners, printers, and cathode-ray screens. And there is the analog-computer industry, whose 1963 volume was around $45 million and whose sales are growing at better than 15 per cent a year. The analog, unlike the digital computer does not count sequentially and has no memory, but it compares many quantities simultaneously, and so provides a swift way of looking at a complex system all at once, in real time. It is indispensable in such jobs as military fire control, and is much used in simulation. The I.B.M. of the analog-computer industry is Electronics Associates of Long Branch, New Jersey, which in 1963 earned about $2,200,000 on $29 million sales. Some others in the field are Beckman Instruments, Veeder-Root, and Westinghouse.

THE SOFTWARE INDUSTRY

Even more dynamic than the industry's fringe hardware producers are its dozens if not hundreds of software and service companies, which sell machine time, prepare special programs and compilers (or general programs), and dispense management advice, particularly in systems work. This market, estimated at some $1.5 billion for 1964, is perhaps three-quarters accounted for by the computer manufacturers themselves, and at least three-quarters of *their* software is necessarily accounted for by I.B.M. Of the $250 million to $400 million left to the "independents," furthermore, I.B.M.'s Service Bureau Corporation takes more than $50 million. The other "independents," however, are prospering, and look forward to growing faster than the computer industry itself. Four of the most important commercial software companies are:

• C-E-I-R (formerly Corporation for Economic & Industrial Research) of Arlington, Virginia, founded in 1954, went into too many fields and made the mistake of buying too much equipment. Having sold it all and leased it back and so bucked up its working capital, it is now striving for profitability. Sales in 1963 were $18 million.

• Computer Usage Company of New York, one of the oldest of the group, was founded in 1955 by John Sheldon and Elmer Kubie, both formerly with I.B.M. They have increased sales 50 per cent every year; in 1963 sales were $3 million, net was $126,000.

• Computer Applications of New York, founded in 1960, is headed by another ex-I.B.M. man named John DeVries. Revenues in 1963 were $2,800,000 and net was $154,000.

• Computer Sciences Corporation of El Segundo, California, was founded in 1959 by Fletcher Jones, who a decade ago was a programmer at North American Aviation. Sales in 1963 were $3,300,000, and net was $392,000. Jones predicts that at least one $100-million software company will emerge from the bunch, his included.

Software companies face a certain threat in the computer manufacturers' drive to make machines more compatible and in their practice of providing more software. But this does not worry most software people. For one thing, says Jones, manufacturers still call on the independents for help, and probably will keep on doing so. For another, the needs and demands of computer buyers and renters are growing even faster than their numbers. Some can't afford their own programmers, whose high salaries can upset internal salary schedules. And anyway their needs fluctuate too much to justify a staff of programmers large enough for peak demand.

What is more important, almost every application opens the door to a world of possibilities, and even the most perceptive and knowledgeable have hardly begun to grasp them all. The potentialities of the computer, unlike the potentialities of other machines, are almost human in their expansibility and variety. What the genius four years of age is to the same person of twenty-four, today's computer applications will be to those twenty years hence. It is the awareness of this dazzling and yet half-veiled promise that makes the computer business so exhilarating to those who are putting everything they have into it.

5

Management May Never Be the Same Again

ONE HORROR STORY making the rounds in the data-processing world tells of a new centralized computer system that delivered divisional operating results to the executive suite before the division managers themselves received the tidings. The company's sadistic president, to show these poor middle managers how superfluous the computer had made them, called them in and harassed them about the data they had not yet seen. The story is probably apocryphal, and certainly should be; but it suggests tolerably well the momentous change that is overtaking the art and science of management as computers become more widely used.

The change is most visible in middle management. Because the computer replaces manpower directly and enables other machines to replace more, it is perhaps the most powerful tool for raising human productivity ever invented, and automatically does away with many supervisory jobs. What may be more consequential, it is changing subordinate management's tasks by eliminating many time-honored functions, such as those of bookkeepers, and by creating many new ones, particularly jobs for systems men with special skills in applying the computer to management science. Some corporations, though loath to discuss the effects of the computer for quotation, regard the displacement of middle management as a harder and more persistent problem than the displacement of line employees, and farsighted ones are thinking in terms of management retraining programs.

But the most important change, because it is basically responsible for all others, is the change at the top. As the power plant of the new so-called information technology, the computer is steadily raising high management's power to make accurate decisions. The world has immemorially underestimated the order of talent needed to run a complex business, particularly a highly competitive enterprise. Compared to the relatively formal problems normally encountered by engineers, physicists, and even medicos, the problems confronting the high corporate executive are gnarled and ill structured. Wherever he looks deeply, he gazes into uncertainty. About the future of the economy he must take the word of soothsayers who usually have been 100 per cent right mainly when explaining why the other fellow was wrong. He can spend millions to find out precisely what the public wants, only to watch his brave new product flop ignominiously. He may know 786 employees by their first names, but just when he thinks everything at home is proceeding according to plan, some division manager makes another $10-million mistake.

The great achievement of the computer is that it is enabling the executive to clear away some of the uncertainty that surrounds him, to subtract some of the variables from the circumstances that fret him, to convert many ill-structured and inherently insoluble problems into well-structured and partly soluble ones, to rely less on hunches and intuition and more on analysis, to behave less like an artist and more like a scientist in disposing of routine matters, and to save his creativity and imagination for more important work.

THE WORD IS RECENTRALIZE

The machine's power to help U.S. managers control their operations has generated what appears to be nothing less than a pervasive recentralization or reintegration movement. For twenty-five years or so decentralization has been the word for corporations all over the world, and the reason seems obvious enough. As companies grew larger and more complex or more diversified, one man or a small group was no longer able to run them directly. So top managers broke down their organizations functionally, and delegated authority to divisional managers, who were often assigned divisional profit goals, enhanced perhaps by profit sharing.

The most resplendent example of decentralization doubtless has been the world's largest corporation, General Motors, whose development of decentralized operations and centralized policy was chronicled by Alfred P. Sloan, Jr., in his recent best-seller, *My Years with General Motors.* But as one observer has remarked, General Motors decentralized so successfully that it has functioned almost as smoothly as a small homogeneous company. What he meant was that the ideal administrative setup is provided by the small tight company, in which one man knows everything that is going on and can make all the decisions without cutting red tape, when and as he thinks best. If decentralization was a historical necessity it was also something of a necessary evil, the tribute that a big organization had to pay to the economies of "scale," i.e., mass production. Most decentralization has been successful. But the near disaster of General Dynamics, which in 1960–1961 suffered a loss of $425 million, the biggest in the history of private enterprise, testifies that making decentralization work is not easy. The General Dynamics case also testifies eloquently that the top managers of a big company justify themselves to their stockholders and the world only if they can and do manage.

A fundamental reason why one man or a few men could not control large decentralized companies was that the science of gathering and passing on information was not far enough advanced. This is no longer true. In the words of Herbert Simon, professor of administration at the Graduate School of Industrial Administration at Carnegie Tech, just as the cable and wireless once brought farflung and quasi-autonomous ambassadors and proconsuls under home-office control, so the computer is now radically altering the balance of advantage between centralization and decentralization. It organizes and processes information so swiftly that computerized information systems enable top management to know everything important that happens as soon as it happens in the largest and most dispersed organizations. The general staff can bypass many intermediate functionaries, dispense with much subordinate judgment, and even plan and create for the whole organization by using the computer to simulate the company's activities in dozens or hundreds of hypothetical situations in order to choose the best course. The problem is not how to get information to the top, but how to keep useless information from coming to the top, how to decide on the "exception" information that management needs to act effectively. That problem, as we shall see, is being solved handily. At all events, whenever a decentralized company has used the computer to automate operations, and particularly when it has installed management information systems, it has willy-nilly found itself behaving more like a centralized company.

Recently General Motors itself stirred up systems men with an announcement that it will computerize its worldwide communication system, which connects all G.M.'s far-flung activities with Detroit. The network, a Control Data 8050 system, will be used to order autos and parts, to help control inventories and production, and to keep Detroit *au courant* with everything relevant happening everywhere. Systems specialists promptly concluded that this was the first step in creating a huge management information system. G.M. insists that its policy is to remain decentralized; the new network is strictly for communications, and will make for better, not more, control. However, some of G.M.'s divisions, which are huge corporations in their own right, are moving toward centralization by building up integrated data systems of their own. One expert who has observed similar developments in other companies predicts that G.M. will inevitably find itself pulling its automotive divisions more tightly together.

"SOMETHING IS HAPPENING TO DECENTRALIZATION"

An outstanding example of the trend is Standard Oil Company (N.J.), the world's No. 2 corporation. As a holding company that owns all or a majority of the stock of more than 200 "affiliates," Jersey has been a textbook example of a company that lives by a policy of decentralization. Each affiliate has its own board of directors and officers, and the parent company nominally "coordinates" the efforts of those affiliates. Actually, the word "coordinate" has been increasingly a euphemism for "control," which many companies, particularly international operators, understandably prefer not to use. Among other things, Jersey has always performed the very important *operation* of directing and allocating the flow of petroleum products among its affiliates. In this job the computer proved indispensable years ago, and since then the machine has made possible a good deal more coordination and standardization of operating practices. "As we minimize differences," said a Jersey official in a symposium sponsored by Chicago's Graduate School of Business and the McKinsey Foundation back in 1959, "something is happening to the concept of decentralization . . . Why should it continue? Obviously the answer is not so simple, particularly since decentralization has become so institutionalized and will create pressures for its retention. Change must await technological developments."

Some of those developments have arrived, and many are on the way. To decide just what should go into a management information system, Melvin Grosz, Jersey's painstaking assistant controller and head of its computer systems department, has developed what he calls an Objectives Decomposition Method, or a way of decomposing or analyzing management information requirements. "We've already discovered," says Grosz, "that most decisions people consider intuitive today can be found to have an underlying structure if you work long enough." For three years, using this method, Grosz and his staff have been building up what they call a Uniform Reporting System, and in two years hope to have it transmitting all the important information the company's coordinators will need to cope with the world at large, including forecasts of supply and demand and of financial conditions. Even today the affiliates are kept in line by the computer. Although each affiliate develops its own operating and long-range plans, New York must decide what will be the best combination for the company as a whole. Therefore it appraises the plans by simulation and passes on them accordingly.

International Harvester also has been known as a decentralized company. But its Systems and Data Service Department, which enjoys the prestige of a major department, has acquired a reputation for doing very "advanced" work, and Harvester in effect has been recentralizing. "If you originally decentralized to give responsibility and profit control to a certain level and you are getting good performance," says John DeMots, manager of Harvester's systems department, "why then you may have no reason for recentralization. But if you decentralized because you lacked information to make timely informed decisions to command and control your organization—if you hadn't time to make the decision centrally and also make it effective—you centralize. Vertically as well as laterally, we think we have achieved a substantial integration of information. And we're just starting."

One of the most ambitious computerized information systems anywhere is being installed at Mead Corporation, sixth in the paper industry, under Vice-President Richard Gilbert, formerly head systems man with McDonnell Aircraft. Mead is a disparate company, with seventeen operations making wood pulp, various kinds of paper, paperboard, and containers. Accordingly, it has been highly decentralized. In 1961 the company, on the advice of its accountant, Touche, Ross, Bailey & Smart, decided to install a "total" system that would include not only process control but a real-time management information system—i.e., one that delivers information in time to do something about it. This system, though unfinished, is already tightening up on efficiency, mainly by centralizing primary planning and control.

"When I first came to Mead," says Gilbert, "each plant operated with its own data-processing system and bought its own equipment. Now we have coordinated the divisions in systems work and in equipment purchases; everything ties in with the total system. We are thus able to centralize corporate planning functions. At the same time we will measure the performance of various divisions against the corporate plan and provide the information that will let them follow it. We will set the limits but, of course, we will not tell a manager how to run a plant. We will centralize the essential things, such as scheduling; but if there is a power failure or flood the mill manager must have the flexibility to take action as he sees best."

Not to be outdone, International Paper, largest in the industry, more recently announced that it will set up what it describes as the most comprehensive information and control system ever undertaken in the paper business. I.P. will expand its present computer installations with "nearly a score" of I.B.M. 360 machines, complete with visual-display units; thus it will create an integrated system that will both control papermaking processes and provide on-line information to the company's manufacturing, financial, scientific, and marketing functions.

MORE HIERARCHICAL THAN EVER?

There is a certain amount of disagreement about just how far recentralization will go and what will happen to it over the long run. A few management experts have argued that computerization would result in more decentralization because subordinate managers, the men on the spot, could use their own computers to make better decisions than anyone else. This argument, though, has largely run aground on the fact that centralized computer systems have already saved millions by company-wide integration of such functions as purchasing, inventory control, and scheduling. Another argument goes that responsibility for making money endows subordinate managers with unusual drive, and that computerized recentralization will destroy this valuable asset. The case has some merit, but with important qualifications. If subordinate managers with responsibility have shown commendable drive, they have frequently cherished "subgoals" that have not necessarily coincided with the goals of the company as a whole. Experience already suggests that discreet monitoring of their activities by computer systems makes them more sensitive to the company's goals. And if, as many students of management wisely argue, the job of high management is to advise and help rather than boss subordinate managers, it can do so only if it knows a great deal about the work of the man being advised.

Always making allowances for the fact that circumstances alter cases, some insist that the combination of highly centralized *policy* control and a certain amount of decentralized *operating* authority is feasible and desirable. U.S. Steel, which has been regarded as a classic example of too much decentralization, is now recentralizing drastically, consolidating seven operating divisions, closing twenty-five sales offices, and coordinating sales and research. But it is also creating five area sales vice-presidents and increasing somewhat the responsibilities of operating and sales middle managers. Norman Ream, head of Lockheed's systems department, believes that management "philosophy" should govern the degree of centralization. He also thinks that high management's new ability to control a lot of activities may make for more decentralization of a kind; companies will be more inclined to diversify or to move into products wholly different from their regular line in order to even out cyclical sales fluctuations.

Looking further into the future, Thomas Whisler of the University of Chicago's Graduate School of Business, whose specialty is studying the effect of new technology on business, theorizes that top management will be composed more than ever of formally educated professionals, who as such may not be as organization-minded as today's executives. Thus the corporate high command might become less a military hierarchy and more a partnership. Operations may be centered in the computer, Whisler explains, and creative managerial functions distributed among professional specialists. But he has no clear idea of how this might come about. Meantime, he agrees with those who believe that the computer is centralizing control, and that the management structure of corporations will be hardly less hierarchical than it is now.

"HIS INTUITION WASN'T GOOD ENOUGH"

Much of the information at the top manager's disposal has been too inaccurate, incomplete, and untimely for well-structured, analytical reasoning. Partly because of this, he has needed a high talent for intuitive judgment, or for assaying variables and unknowns (as women are supposed to) by rules of thumb, shrewd guesses, and sharp feelings. The computer is not only enabling but forcing him to think more explicitly and analytically—to formalize his decision-making process and spell out his judgments.

The machine can even show up defects in his problem solving. "Nothing is more ill-defined than the way some managers arrive at their decisions," comments a systems man. "One day one of our managers gave me a question he said the computer couldn't solve: 'If two large machines are to be delivered to separate customers on February 1 and I have only one machine on that date, which customer do I ship to?' My answer was that if he told me the process by which *he* arrived at his decision, we could instruct the computer to go through the same process. The trouble with that manager, we soon found out, was that he never knew *how* he arrived at his decisions, and his intuition wasn't good enough to keep him from making mistakes."

The top manager is rapidly discovering that he has to take a deep and continuous interest in the computer, in working closely with systems men, in overcoming middle-management resistance, and in measuring results. Too many, in the past, have turned the whole "mess" over to a subordinate and forgotten about it. The subordinate, when he found out what could be done with the computer, necessarily began to monkey with the company's structure, job functions, and basic ways of doing business. Unless the top executive knows what the subordinate is doing and why, crises are inevitable. Thomas Whisler tells of one controller who had installed computer applications that were largely responsible for turning red ink into black, and had streamlined the company's whole structure. The president, who did not know what was going on and hardly knew a computer from a water cooler, had meanwhile brought in some ambitious young men to replace retiring division heads. As a result of the ensuing collision between the new division heads and the systems people, the company wallowed in turmoil, and its computer program was stalled for two years.

Thanks to the computer's ability to monitor, officers of large and disparate companies are finding it profitable to take a more thoroughgoing interest in their operations than they ever have, and without spending an undue amount of time on them. For several years now Westinghouse has been showing poor profit margins. In a resolute drive to improve the company's productivity, President Donald Burnham, using his computerized management information system to diagnose weaknesses and cut costs, has reduced the white-collar staff by some 4,000, including a lot of middle managers.

The computer system in another company showed that inventory in one large division had begun to rise inordinately, to around $100 million, and looked as if it might get out of control. The president immediately took an interest. "We asked the guy in charge if that was a valid inventory picture," he says, "and he agreed it was. We said it looked about $30 million too high, but he replied that he had an enthusiastic bunch of salesmen who he thought could get rid of the stuff. This attitude was O.K., but the overstock held on for four months. That manager is no longer with us."

MANY DICE, EACH WITH A HUNDRED SIDES

This new mastery of operations gives—or should give—top management more time for its *strategic* work, such as long-range planning, policy making, choosing staff, deciding on new products and capital investments, financing, and public and labor relations. All computer-systems men worth their salt have learned that top management does not need the detailed, day-to-day information that is proving so valuable to subordinate managers. To keep their top executives from being inundated with useless (if interesting) paper, they are striving to provide them only with the "exception" operating information that demands or justifies action. The systems departments of several companies, notably Jersey and Chrysler, are engaged in analyzing exactly what their staff executives do, and what information they now need and are likely to need as the supply of relevant facts increases. What is more, computer-systems men are working hard to help management cope with the baffling variables of the outside world and to master the strategic problems of planning.

One of the important planning tools is simulation, which, as we have seen, allows managers to test the effect of alternative courses. When an executive is trying to make up his mind, he weighs pros and cons and estimates or guesses on the odds in his favor; simulation simply expands and formalizes this process far beyond the power of any human mind. Nothing is attended with more uncertainty than the process of deciding on expansion and capital investment; as David Hertz of McKinsey & Company has remarked, it is like trying to predict the outcome of a game played with many dice, each with a hundred sides. Hertz has worked out an ingenious simulation process that considers as many as forty variables, such as market size, selling price, market growth rate, share of market, investment required. With the computer he works out the odds on these variables and the likeliest combinations of them; and by repeating the process of selection and computation he arrives at the best bet.

Similar if less sophisticated methods are being used by dozens of companies. Westinghouse employs an alternative investment routine that rates projects by yield and time required to produce the yield, and relates them to the capital available. Much depends on the estimates of return made by the division managers, and part of the technique is to appraise the judgment of division managers. "Five years from now," says Lou Hague, director of business systems, "we'll be able to say manager A has made investments that were right 93 per cent of the time, while manager B has a rating of 72 per cent, and such ratings will help our line management make the final decisions." Trying to reduce the uncertainty in assaying its external environment, Westinghouse is also building up a store of what it calls Directive and Environmental Information, covering employees, stockholders, customers, government, and the economy. "We are working on a simulation of the company in the real world," explains Hague. "It's a tough job, but that isn't stopping us."

Some companies have begun to use the computer in marketing—not merely for processing orders, but for sales forecasting, distribution planning, pricing, and even for buying advertising space. "We are learning how to gauge the market," says International Harvester's John DeMots. "For the first time we know 90 per cent of what we sell within a few days. We try not only to forecast broad trends but to figure out what industry volume and our own volume will be. Our sales manager, as a result, is channeling his and his staff's energy more effectively."

UNCERTAINTY IS INFINITE

Such advances, computer people believe, will eventually be followed by systems that will command enough pertinent information to answer almost any relevant question put to them. "The corporate planning technique," predicts Whisler, "will then become one of creative interrogation." An elaborate demonstration of how creative interrogation would work occurred May 4, 1964, at Fort Wayne, Indiana, when representatives of several companies attended a demonstration of a computerized management information device staged by Information Management Facilities, Inc. In response to requests from "managers" in the audience, the computer displayed its answers, in color and sometimes in chart form, on a screen wall. The hypothetical situation: a $100 million appliance corporation experienced a sudden decline in air-conditioning sales and a drop in profit margin, and the problem was how to bring the margin back to normal. The "managers" called for relevant information, such as projection of sales requirements to meet certain profit levels, results of new market tests, and data on efficiency of various plants; and the exercise culminated in a decision to close down a certain plant. Given a computer with enough information, such a system could not only save untold hours of expensive paper shuffling in the decision-making process, but also generate decisions with more logic behind them. At least two large corporations are installing display systems; one manufacturer of display equipment, predicts that within five years more than 1,000 civilian management information systems will be using perhaps 10,000 units.

Thus the job of top manager will be at once easier and harder. He will be faced with less uncertainty in the sense that he will know more about what is going on, but he will have to think harder and more precisely to take advantage of his knowledge. He will have more time for creative interrogation and long-range strategy; but this will be little if any easier than it is now. Though he will make more analytical judgments, he will need his intuition as much as ever, for ignorance and uncertainty are infinite as space itself, and there will always be plenty to guess about. Moreover, a large part of every such manager's job will always be concerned with human relations, and he must present a figure of esteem to a world whose judgments are heavily charged with emotion. All these time-tested faculties and virtues, however, will avail him little if he does not understand how to use the new management tools at his disposal.

THE SURVIVORS AND THRIVERS

The middle and lower orders of managers seem in for a stormy time. Now middle management is an unavoidably imprecise term, covering very different jobs in different companies; but as a rule it includes all managers below the highest policy level, sometimes even vice presidents. Nearly seven years ago, in what is something of a classic among systems people, Thomas Whisler with Harold J. Leavitt (now of Carnegie Tech) published in the *Harvard Business Review* several speculations on how the new information technology, powered by the computer, would affect management in the 1980s. Among their many prognostications, most of which seem to be turning out well, were two about middle management: (1) its ranks would be reduced, and business organization structures would consequently be "flattened"; and (2) many middle-management functions would be routinized, downgrading many middle managers.

The first of the two predictions seems to be coming true. The number of middle-management jobs relative to output appears to be declining, and for several reasons. One is that white-collar jobs, apparently owing to the computer, are not increasing nearly as fast as they did. Between 1950 and 1960 the average increase was 2.8 per cent a year but in 1963 it was less than 1 per cent. All this probably means fewer supervisory jobs.

The computer is also displacing a lot of middle management by forcing companies to change the nature of the jobs they offer. Since accounting is often being done by computer as part of systems work, many bookkeeping departments as such are virtually being eliminated, and accountants are being forced into systems work and cost and financial analysis. Functions like credit management, warehouse management, and even sales have been consolidated. One firm, says Thomas Whisler, reduced the number of managerial positions in several divisions by 30 per cent in two years. But he notes that this kind of structural flattening is often accompanied by recombination of parts of former jobs into new bundles of responsibility. And "as you might expect, when the smoke of these reorganizations died away, the managers who survived and thrived were those who saw the advantage of this new system early."

The prediction that many middle-management positions would be routinized or degraded does not seem to be coming off, at least not yet. In some places intermediate managers are being thoroughly monitored by the computer; Lockheed's ADA data-collection system, discussed in a previous chapter, prevents supervisors from indulging in "load balancing," or the practice of transferring some work done from one day to another in daily reports, thus concealing the true capacity of their departments. Westinghouse's experience has been similar. Before installing data-gathering equipment, Westinghouse rated one factory's production at 85 per cent; after the equipment was installed, the load balancing was discovered, and the plant was rated at 45 per cent; now it is at a true 80 per cent.

Checking up on supervisory management, however, is not quite the same as routinizing or degrading it, and it is hard to come up with specific examples of the latter. What happens, Whisler theorizes, is that a good deal of the average middle manager's job is ordinarily given over to communicating with customers, colleagues, employees; and the computer, by relieving him of the necessity of valuing all information that comes his way, is freeing him for other profitable activities. "Much middle management," predicts Norman Ream, "will change from clerical and advisory work to short-range planning, in order to free top management for long-range planning."

Nevertheless, the computer is upsetting functions, displacing men, and wiping out jobs, and it consequently is generating fear and resistance in middle management. This is one reason why top officers and systems men often prefer not to discuss the effects of the computer realistically; and why company systems men, who must of course secure the cooperation of their own middle managers, allude to these men almost deferentially as their customers. A supervisor who has devoted his life to running a department that has become obsolete can be the hardest man of all to shift, and this is why the realization is growing that displacement of middle managers may be a harder and more persistent problem than the displacement of blue- and white-collar employees.

If some enthusiasts are right, more adjustments are in the offing. The day will soon come, they say, when computers will be instructed to make decisions "heuristically," i.e., by using rules of thumb and reasoning in terms of means and ends; thus the machines will gradually be able to solve not only well-structured but badly structured problems, and so will be able to make many decisions now made by middle management. Carnegie Tech's Herbert Simon argues that most decisions governing routine day-to-day physical operation of companies will be programmed and automated.

TOMORROW'S MANAGERS

Now for the other side of the coin. Some ranks of middle management are being swollen by computer and systems men ranging all the way from programmers to specialists in such esoteric techniques as PERT and operations research.

They are in short supply everywhere; the metropolitan Sunday papers contain pages of advertisements offering high rewards for their talents. These systems people are young, and a large percentage have advanced degrees; many are qualifying for more important jobs. "We look for broader interests," says Richard Gilbert. "Some of our analysts are very able and don't want to be operations research people all their lives."

Will these people fill a large percentage of tomorrow's top-management posts? In the past forty years a large part of high corporate manpower has been supplied by legal and financial talent, and for obvious reasons. Although these specialists had to master detail, they also had to take a broad, spacious view of problems in order to understand and rationalize their companies' role in the economy. Roger Blough of U.S. Steel is a good example; as a young Wall Street lawyer assigned in the 1930s to defend U.S. Steel against the charges of the Temporary National Economic Committee's investigation of "bigness," Blough learned so much about the industry, both in detail and in the round, that he was soon chief legal talent for the company, and was bound for bigger things.

The higher order of systems and computer people should be in an even better position to know about the business than lawyers and treasurers were. They will have to understand the company's operating techniques and its relationships with the outside world, and they will have to take both an analytical and a creative attitude toward them. "We think," says John DeMots, "we can bring in a young man and assign him to help design several systems, and teach him more about the business than in any other way." Although the ranks of computer-systems men contain a lot of men who seem "bloodless" and excessively engrossed in the technicalities of their indubitably fascinating business, some have already ascended to high management posts. The law of averages and their own intellectual growth should take care of others. The computerized world will be an oyster for the young man with brains, judgment, imagination, personality, education, ambition—and a good knowledge of computers.

6

Will the Computer Outwit Man?

Ever since it emerged from the mists of time, the human race has been haunted by the notion that man-made devices might overwhelm and even destroy man himself. The sorcerer's apprentice who almost drowned his world, Frankenstein's frustrated monster who tortured and destroyed his creator, the androids that mimic human beings in the frenzied pages of today's science fiction magazines—all play upon the age-old fear that man's arrogant mind will overleap itself. And now comes the electronic computer, the first invention to exhibit something of what in human beings is called intelligence. Not only is the computer expanding man's brainpower, but its own faculties are being expanded by so-called artificial intelligence; and the machine is accordingly endowing man's ancient fears with a reality and immediacy no other invention ever has.

The fears are several and intricately related, but three major ones encompass the lot. The one that worries the columnists and commentators is that the computer will hoist unemployment so intolerably that the free-enterprise system will be unable to cope with the problem, and that the government will have to intervene on a massive scale. This belief, so noisily espoused by offbeat groups like the Ad Hoc Committee on the Triple Revolution, has already been dealt with in this series. It is enough to repeat here that the computer will doubtless go down in history not as the explosion that blew unemployment through the roof, but as the technological triumph that enabled the U.S. economy to maintain the secular growth rate on which its greatness depends.

The second fear is that the computer will eventually become so intelligent and even creative that it will relegate man, or most men, to a humiliating and intolerably inferior role in the world. This notion is based on the fact that the computer already can learn (after a fashion), can show purposeful behavior (narrowly defined), can sometimes act "creatively" or in a way its programmer does not expect it to—and on the probability that artificial-intelligence research will improve it enormously on all three counts. Meanwhile there is the third fear, which is that the computer's ability to make certain neat, clean decisions will beguile men into abdicating their capacity and obligation to make the important decisions, including moral and social ones. This fear as such would be academic if the second one were realized; for if the computer ever betters man's brainpower (broadly defined), then its judgments will be superior too and men finally will be outwitted. To appraise both fears, therefore, we must examine artificial-intelligence research, the formidable new science that is striving so industriously to make the computer behave like a human being.

THE ROUTES TO JUDGMENT

The goal of artificial-intelligence research is to write programs or sets of instructions showing the computer how to behave in a way that in human beings would be called intelligent.* The workers proceed on the assumption that human nervous systems process information in the act of thinking; and that given enough observation, experiment, analysis, and modeling, they can instruct a digital computer to process information as humans do. Broadly speaking, they simulate human intelligence in two ways. One is to build actual counterparts of the brain or the nervous systems with computer-controlled models of neural networks. The other and more productive approach (so far) is to analyze problems that can be solved by human intelligence and to write a computer program that will solve the problems. Most if not all their toil involves programming the computer "heuristically"—that is, showing it how to use rules of thumb, to explore the likeliest paths, and to make educated guesses in coming to a conclusion, rather than running through all the alternatives to find the right one. Looking closely at their ingenious achievements, which appear so marvelous to the layman, one begins to understand why it is easy to make sweeping projections of the machine's future as an intelligent mechanism.

But these research workers have a hard if exhilarating time ahead of them. When one turns to living intelligence, one is struck with the colossal job that remains to be done—if the word "job" is not too presumptuous to be used in this context at all. If one defines intelligence merely as the ability

* Many researchers shudder at the phrase "artificial intelligence." Its anthropomorphic overtones, they say, often arouse irrelevant emotional responses—i.e., in people who think it sacrilegious to try to imitate the brain.

to adjust to environment, the world is positively quivering with what might be called extracomputer intelligence. Even the lowest species can reproduce and live without instruction by man, something no computer can do. Moreover, the exercise of intelligence in animals, and particularly in higher animals, is a stupendously complex process. As Oliver Selfridge and Ulric Neisser of M.I.T. have put it in a discussion of human pattern recognition, man is continually confronted with a welter of data from which he must pick patterns relevant to whatever he is doing at the time. "A man who abstracts a pattern from a complex of stimuli has essentially classified the possible inputs," they write. "But very often the basis of his classification is unknown even to himself; it is too complex to be specified explicitly."

Yet specify the researcher must if he is to simulate human behavior in the machine. For the electronic computer is a device that processes or improves data according to a program or set of instructions. Since it is equipped with a storage or memory, a stored program, and a so-called conditional transfer, which permits it to make choices, it can be instructed to compare and assess and then judge. Nevertheless its conclusions are the logical consequences of the data and program fed into it; and it still must be told not merely what to do, but how, and the rules must be written in minute and comprehensive detail. Ordinary programs contain thousands of instructions. The research worker cannot make the machine do anything "original" until he has painstakingly instructed it how to be original, and thus its performance, at bottom, depends on the intelligence or even genius of its preceptor.

Although the men doing artificial-intelligence research are themselves extraordinarily intelligent, they disagree widely and acrimoniously not only about what exactly they expect to do but even about what exactly they have done. In a recent paper John Kelly of Bell Laboratories and M.I.T.'s Selfridge, who between themselves disagree about almost everything, agreed that the most controversial subject in this work is whether man's ability to form concepts and to generalize, an age-old concern of philosophers, can ever be imitated. Some conservative extremists think no machines can ever emulate this faculty, while their opposites believe the problem is about to be solved. The moderates take various stands in between.

Everybody in the intelligence business would probably agree with Kelly and Selfridge that the task of simulating human intelligence has a long way to go. "Our position may be compared to pioneers on the edge of a new continent," they write. "We have tested our axes on twigs, and made ladders and boats of paper. In principle we can cut down any tree, but obviously trees several miles in girth will take discouragingly long. We can span any river with bridges or boats in principle, but if the river is an Amazon with a thirty-knot current we may not be able to do it in fact. Then again, the continent may be two light years across. However, as pioneers, what we do *not* see is a river of molten lava, which at one sight would make us admit the inapplicability of our tools."

THE MACHINE THAT LEARNS

One man who has chopped more than a few twigs and crossed a stream or two, but has no illusions about the rivers and forests ahead, is Arthur Samuel, consultant to I.B.M.'s director of research. Samuel, who has been classified as close to center in the field of intelligence research, pioneered in machine learning in the late 1950s by teaching a computer to play checkers so well that it now consistently beats him. To program the machine to play the game, Samuel in effect stored a model of the checkerboard in the computer. Then he instructed the machine to look ahead as a person does, and to consider each move by analyzing the opponent's possible replies and counter-replies. Although the machine theoretically could search *all* possible choices, there are 10^{40} such choices in every game; and even the fastest computer would take longer than many think the universe is old to play a game by ticking off them all.

So Samuel instructed the machine to proceed heuristically by feeding it two "routines" that showed it how to learn from experience. One routine told it how to remember past positions and their outcomes, and the other told it how to improve the way it appraises positions. The machine got steadily better, and was soon superior to its master. But this does not mean, Samuel insists, that the computer is categorically superior to man. It beats him not because it uses information or techniques unknown or unknowable to man, but simply because its infallible memory, fantastic accuracy, and prodigious speed allow it to make a detailed but unimaginative analysis in a few seconds that would take man years to make. When, if, and as a championship chess program is constructed, says Samuel, the same generalization will hold. No chess program can yet play much better than an advanced novice; the reason is that chess is vastly more complex than checkers, and nobody has yet devoted enough time or thought to the task.

The limitations of the computer, Samuel likes to point out, are not in the machine but in man. To make machines that appear to be smarter than man, man himself must be smarter than the machine; more explicitly, "A higher order of intelligence, or at least of understanding, seems required to instruct a machine in the art of being intelligent than is required to duplicate the intelligence the machine is to simulate."

Samuel scoffs at the notion that the great things in store for the machine will give it a will, properly defined, of its own. In relatively few years machines that learn from experience will be common. The development of input and output devices has some way to go, but in twenty years or so businessmen may be able to discuss tasks and problems with computers almost as they now discuss them with other employees; and televideo-phones, for companies that cannot afford their own computer systems, will make central machines as convenient as the telephone itself. Programs will be written to instruct machines to modify their own rules, or to modify the *way* they modify rules, and so on; and programs will also instruct one machine to program another, and even how to design and construct a second and more powerful machine. However, Samuel insists, the machine will not and cannot do any of these things until it has been shown how to proceed; and to understand how to do this, man will have to develop still greater understanding. As the great originator, he will necessarily be on top.

THE ARTIFICIAL BRAIN

An *apparent* exception to such a conclusion, Samuel acknowledges, is that man may eventually build a machine as complex as the brain, and one that will act independently of him. The human brain, which contains roughly 10 billion cells called neurons, works strikingly like a computer because its neurons react or "fire" by transmitting "excitatory" or "inhibitory" electrical impulses to other neurons. Each neuron is connected to 100 others on the average, and sometimes to as many as 10,000, and each presumably gets more than one signal before "firing." Whether these neurons are at birth connected at random or in a kind of pattern nobody knows, but learning, most research workers think, has something to do with changes in the strength and number of the connections. Some hold that creativity in human beings consists of "an unextinguishable core of randomness," i.e., creative people possess a lot of random connections.

To imitate the behavior of neurons, several researchers have built "self-learning" or "adaptive" machines using mechanical, electrical, and even chemical circuits, whose connections are automatically strengthened, as they presumably are in the brain, by successful responses. The Perceptron, built by Frank Rosenblatt, a Cornell psychologist, has for years been demonstrating that it can improve its ability to recognize numbers and letters of the alphabet by such a routine. Because such devices are proving useful in pattern recognition, they doubtless will be improved.

Theoretically, these techniques might create a monster capable of acting independently of man; but Samuel argues that the brain's complexity makes this highly unlikely. Even if great progress is made in imitating this complexity, not enough is known about the interconnections of the brain to construct a reasonable facsimile thereof; the chance of doing so, Samuel guesses, is about the same as the chance that every American will be stricken with a coronary on the same night. As others have estimated it, moreover, the total cost of duplicating all the brain's cells and connections, even at the ludicrously low cost of only 5 cents per cell and 1 cent per connection, would come to more than $1 quintillion, or $1 billion billion. Some of the brain's functions can probably be reproduced with vastly fewer cells than the brain contains, however, and the odds on building a tolerably "human" model brain will doubtless improve. But they will improve, Samuel reiterates, only as man improves his understanding of the thinking process; and his ability to control the mechanical brain will increase to the extent he increases his own understanding.

THE OPTIMISTIC EXTREMISTS

Some enthusiastic and optimistic research scientists feel that such judgments tend to understate the potentialities of the machine. Allen Newell and Herbert Simon of the Carnegie Institute of Technology argue that man is no more or less determinate than the computer; he is programmed at birth by his genes, and thenceforth his talents and other traits depend on the way he absorbs and uses life's inputs. The day will come, they prophesy, when a program will enable the machine to do everything, or practically everything, that a man's brain can do. Such a program will not call for "stereotyped and repetitive behavior," but will make the machine's activity "highly conditional on the task environment"—i.e., on the goal set for it, and on the machine's ability to assess its own progress toward that goal.

Meanwhile, Newell and Simon insist, the computer will surpass man in some ways. Back in 1957, Simon formally predicted that within ten years a computer would be crowned the world's chess champion, that it would discover an important new mathematical theorem, that it would write music of esthetic value, and that most theories in psychology would be expressed in computer programs or would take the form of qualitative statements about the properties of such programs. Simon's forecast has only three years to go, but he thinks it still is justified, and he sticks to it. Not only that, he confidently looks forward to the day when computers will be tossing off countless problems too ill-structured for men to solve, and when the machine will even be able to generalize from experience.

Together with Newell and J. C. Shaw of Rand Corporation, Simon has done a great deal of pioneering in artificial intelligence. The trio was one of the first to introduce heuristic methods; and their first notable achievement, in 1956, was the Logic Theory Program, which among other things conjures up proofs for certain types of mathematical and symbolic theorems. It was the Logic Theory Program that independently discovered proofs for some of the theorems in Russell and Whitehead's *Principia Mathematica,* and in at least one instance it provided a shorter and more "elegant" proof than Russell and Whitehead themselves.

Simon and Newell's General Problem Solver, mentioned in the first chapter, is an ambitious feat that instructs the computer to behave adaptively by solving sub-problems before going on to knock off bigger ones, and to reason in terms of means and ends. Using the General Problem Solver, Geoffrey P. E. Clarkson of M.I.T. has successfully instructed a computer to do what an investment trust officer does when he chooses securities for a portfolio. Clarkson analyzed the steps the officer takes, such as appraising the state of the market, and also analyzed these steps according to the postulates of the General Problem Solver. Thereupon Clarkson constructed a program that in several actual tests predicted with astonishing accuracy the trust officer's behavior, down to the names and number of shares chosen for each portfolio. The General Problem Solver, furthermore, aspires to endow computers with more than such problem-solving faculties. It tries to show how people solve problems, and so provide a tool for constructing theories of human thinking. Its techniques, says Simon, "reveal that the free behavior of a reasonably intelligent human can be understood as the product of a complex but finite and determinate set of laws."

One of the most assiduous of the optimists is Marvin Minsky of M.I.T., who believes we are on the threshold of an era that "will quite possibly be dominated by intelligent problem solving machines." Minsky has divided the intelligence research scientists' achievements and problems into five main groups: (1) search, (2) pattern recognition, (3) learning, (4) planning, and (5) induction. To illustrate: in solving a problem, a worker can program a computer to (1) search through any number of possibilities, but because this usually takes too long, it is enormously inefficient. With (2) pattern recognition techniques, however, the worker instructs the machine to restrict itself to important problems; and with (3) learning techniques, he instructs it to generalize on its experience with successful models. With (4) so-called planning methods, he chooses a few from a large number of sub-problems, and instructs the machine to appraise them in several ways. And finally (5) to manage broad problems, he programs the computer to construct models of the world about it; then he tries to program the machine to reason inductively about these models—to discover regularities or "laws of nature," and even to generalize about events beyond its recorded experience.

Minsky has predicted that in thirty years the computer will in many ways be smarter than men, but he concedes that the machine will achieve this high state only after very smart men have worked very long hours. "In ten years," he says, "we may have something with which we can carry on a reasonable conversation. If we work hard, we may have it in five; if we loaf, we may never have it."

WHAT IS SUSIE TO JOE?

Merely to describe briefly the artificial-intelligence projects now under way would take volumes. Among the more important are question-answering programs that allow a computer to be interrogated in English: the so-called BASEBALL project at M.I.T.'s Lincoln Laboratory, which answers a variety of queries about American League teams; and the SAD SAM (Sentence Appraiser and Diagrammer–Semantic Analyzer Machine) program of Robert Lindsay of the University of Texas, which constructs a model of a family and tells the computer how to reply to queries about family relationships, such as "How is Susie Smith related to Joe and Oscar Brown, and how are the two Browns related?"

There is Oliver Selfridge's pioneering work in pattern recognition, which has led to techniques that have progressed from recognizing simple optical characters like shapes to recognizing voices. Pattern recognition, in turn, leads to the simulation of verbal learning behavior; one program that does this is the Elementary Perceiver and Memorizer (EPAM) of Herbert Simon and Edward A. Feigenbaum of the University of California. EPAM provides a model for information processes that underlie man's power to acquire, differentiate, and relate elementary symbolic material like single syllables; and it has been used to compare computer behavior with human behavior and to construct "adaptive" pattern recognition models. So far, so good. But the human brain forms concepts as well as recognizing digits and words; and although some work is being done on programming a model of human concept formulation, relatively little progress has been made in telling a machine just how to form concepts and to generalize as people do. And as we have already noted, there is much disagreement about the degree of even that progress.

THE IMPEDIMENTA OF THE INTELLECT

Nobody has yet been able to program the machine to imitate what many competent judges would call true creativity, partly because nobody has yet adequately defined creativity. As a working hypothesis, Newell, Shaw, and Simon have described creativity as a special problem-solving ability characterized by novelty, unconventionality, high persistence, and the power to formulate very difficult problems. This is fine as far as it goes; a creative person may have and indeed probably needs all these. But he willy-nilly brings to his task much more than these purely intellectual aptitudes. He brings a huge impedimentum of basic emotions and aptitudes that were programmed into him congenitally, and have been greatly augmented and modified in a lifetime of conscious and unconscious learning. The terrible temper of his mother's grandfather, his own slightly overactive thyroid and aberrant hypothalamus, his phlegmatic pituitary, his mysterious frustrations, his odd beliefs and prejudices, his phlogistic gonads, his illusions and superstitions, his chronic constipation, his neuroses or psychoses, even the kind of liquor he takes aboard—all these and thousands more combine to color his personality and imagination, and his approach to his work. "No man, within twenty-four hours after having eaten a meal in a Pennsylvania Railroad dining car," H. L. Mencken used to argue, "can conceivably write anything worth reading."

Consider the art of musical composition. "Great music," wrote Paul Elmer More, "is a kind of psychic storm, agitating to fathomless depths the mystery of the past within us." All composers and musicians may not find this a good description—nor may some intelligence research workers—but it suggests strikingly what goes into what a qualified judge would identify as a work of musical art. Such a work is not merely the opus of a brain sealed off in a cranium, but the result of a huge inventory of "states" or influences, inherited or acquired, that has colored that brain's way of performing. The dissimilarities among Dvořák, Mahler, Richard Strauss, and Sibelius, to mention four late romantic composers, are probably the result mainly of obscure inherited and acquired influences. And what dissimilarities they are! Music critics have spent lifetimes and built towering reputations on expounding and appraising just such differences.

The computer's achievements in creative composition, literary and musical, are remarkable in the sense that Dr. Johnson's dog, which could walk on its hind legs, was remarkable: "It is not done well, but you are surprised to find it done at all." Since the vast bulk of durable music is relatively formal, arranged according to rules, it theoretically should be possible to instruct a computer to compose good music. Some have tried. Perhaps the best example of computer music is the Illiac suite, programmed at the University of Illinois. By common consent, the Illiac suite is no great shakes; one of the moderate remarks about it is that repeated hearings tend to induce exasperation. But so, of course, does some "modern" music composed by humans; and it is possible that one day the computer may be programmed to concoct music that many regard as good.

Research workers have had some luck in turning out popular jingles on the computer without a hard, long, expensive struggle; in twenty years or so the computer will doubtless be mass producing ephemeral tunes of the day more cheaply than Tin Pan Alley's geniuses can turn them out. But it appears that instructing a computer to compose deep, complex, or carefully prepared music is an almost heroic task demanding more talent and time (and money) than simply putting the music down in the first place and not bothering with the computer at all.

AUTO-BEATNIK CREATIVITY

Similar observations apply to creative writing. Man as a writer is the human counterpart of the data processor, but the inputs he has stored and the mind he processes them with are the result of thousands of kinds of influences. Put in focus and challenged by the job at hand, his brain processes the relevant data and comes up with all manner of output, from majestic imperative sentences like "No Parking North of Here" (official sign in one large city) to epic poems and novels in the grand style.

It should surprise no one that the computer can be programmed easily and cheaply to do simple jobs of gathering and sorting information, and is in fact doing a rough job of abstracting technical works. As more and more of the world's knowledge is stored on tape or drums, and as centralized retrieval systems are developed, the computer will be able to dredge up nearly everything available on a given subject and arrange it in some kind of order. It will doubtless save much research time, and so prove a boon to writers. The machine, moreover, has already been programmed to write simple-minded television whodunits, and some believe it will soon supply soap opera confectors much of their material, or perhaps eventually convert them into programmers. The cost of using the machine will also pace this "progress"; what the computer and programmer can do more cheaply than the solo word merchant, they will do.

That creative writing of more complexity and depth is something else again is suggested by a sample of "Auto-beatnik" verses "generated" by computers programmed under R. M. Worthy at the Advanced Research Department of General Precision, Inc., Glendale, California. Worthy and his experts have arranged several thousand words into groups, set up sentence patterns and even rhyming rules, and directed the machine to pick words from the groups at random, but in pre-specified order. The computer's verses are syntactically correct but semantically empty; as Worthy allows, a machine must have an environment, a perception, an image, or an "experience" to write a significant sentence. "I am involved in all this nonsense," says Worthy, "because I am fascinated with language. And eventually this research will be valuable in many things like translation and information retrieval." Here is one of the machine's verses:

LAMENT FOR A MONGREL

To belch yet not to boast, that is the hug,
The high lullaby's bay discreetly crushes the bug.
Your science was so minute and hilly,
Yes, I am not the jade organ's leather programmer's recipe.
As she is squealing above the cheroot, these obscure toilets
shall squat,
Moreover, on account of hunger, the room was hot.

A common diversion in computer circles is to speculate on how a programmer would instruct a computer to write as well as Shakespeare. Even the untutored layman can see some of the trees in the forest of problems ahead. Before doing anything, the preceptor must do no less than decide exactly what makes Shakespeare so good, which itself is probably a job for a genius. Then he must write the rules; he must formalize his conclusions about the bard's talents in staggering detail, not omitting even the most trivial implications, so that the machine can proceed logically from one step to another lest it produce elegant gibberish when it starts to "create." The set of instructions or program for such a project would probably run to several times the length of Shakespeare's works. And it might demand more talent than Shakespeare himself possessed.

CREATION AS EFFECTIVE SURPRISE

The indefatigable Newell and Simon, however, are not to be dissuaded. They have speculated on the notion that creativity might not always have to reside in the programmer—that the computer on its own could *match* (not copy) such creations as a Beethoven symphony, *Crime and Punishment*, or a Cezanne landscape. Although they freely admit that no computer has ever come up with an opus approaching any of these, they suggest that none appears to lie beyond computers.

To create, they hold, is to produce effective surprise, not only in others but in the creator; and in principle a computer might do this. "Suppose," they have written, "a computer contains a very large program introduced into it over a long period by different programmers working independently. Suppose that the computer had access to a rich environment of inputs that it has been able to perceive and select from. Suppose—and this is critical—that it is able to make its next step conditional on what it has seen and found, and that it is even able to modify its own program on the basis of past experience, so that it can behave more effectively in the future. At some point, as the complexity of its behavior increases, it may reach a level of richness that produces effective surprise. At that point we shall have to acknowledge that it is creative, or we shall have to change our definition of creativity."

They may. Their definition of creativity, critics feel, may be too narrow because it makes too little allowance for human motivation, or the complex mix of emotions and other drives that compel people to behave as they do. The question is not whether the machine can produce something original; any computer can do something trivial or incomprehensible that nobody has ever done before. The question is whether men can show the machine how to create something that will contain enough human ingredients to meet at least a minimum of approval by perceptive human beings specially qualified to judge the creation. The creations of Newell and Simon's well-educated computer might amount to expensive nonsense unless the computers were fed a vast amount of brilliant instructions on how to handle the sophisticated inputs, and unless these inputs included human motivations.

HUMAN MOTIVATION AND THE COMPUTER

Human motivations, Ulric Neisser believes, must be considered not only by workers who would instruct the machine to create, but also by those who would increase its power otherwise to simulate human intelligence. Man's intelligence, he points out, is not a faculty independent of the rest of human life, and he identifies three important characteristics of human thought that are conspicuously absent from existing or proposed programs: (1) human thought is part of the cumulative process of the growth of the human organism, to which it contributes and on which it feeds; (2) it is inextricably bound up with feelings and emotions, and (3) unlike the computer's behavior, which is single-minded to the exclusion of everything but the problem assigned it, human activity serves many motives at once, even when a person thinks he is concentrating on a single thing. Recent research by George A. Miller of Harvard, Eugene Galanter of Pennsylvania, and Karl Pribram of Stanford suggests that human behavior is much more "hierarchical" and intricately motivated than hitherto assumed, and Neisser thinks that this multiplicity of motives is not a "supplementary heuristic that can be readily incorporated into a problem solving program."

It is man's complex emotional and other drives, in other words, that give his intelligence depth, breadth, and humanity; nobody has yet found a way of programming them into a computer, and Neisser doubts that anybody soon will. He predicts, however, that programming will become vastly more difficult as the machine is used more and more in solving "human" problems. Pattern recognition, learning, and memory will still be research goals, but a harder job will be to inject a measure of human emotion into the machine.

Some feel Neisser errs in suggesting that anybody will want to imitate man's way of thinking in all its complexities. "The computer can and will be programmed to do and be a lot of things," says one research worker, "including acting just as foolishly as any human being." In other words, nobody may want to stuff a machine full of the useless mental impedimenta lugged around by humans; the great merit of the machine is that it can think accurately and single-mindedly, untainted by irrelevant emotions and obscure and even immoral drives.

Nevertheless, the world is populated by human beings, and their motivations cannot be overlooked. For if the computer is asked to solve a problem in which human motivation is important, it will have to be told exactly what that motivation is, and what to do about it and under what circumstances. That will not be easy.

A NEAT, CLEAN, CONSISTENT JUDGMENT

Meanwhile the prospect for instructing the computer to behave like a real human is remote; and this is precisely why some fear that the machine's role as decision maker will be abused. "If machines really thought as men do," Neisser explains, "there would be no more reason to fear them than to fear men. But computer intelligence is not human, it does not grow, has no emotional basis, and is shallowly motivated. These defects do not matter in technical applications, where the criteria for successful problem solving are relatively simple. They become extremely important if the computer is used to make social, business, economic, military, moral and government decisions, for there our criteria of adequacy are as subtle and as multiply motivated as human thinking itself." A human decision maker, he points out, is supposed to do the right thing even in unexpected circumstances, but the computer can be counted on only to deal with the situation anticipated by the programmer.

In a recent issue of *Science,* David L. Johnson of the University of Washington and Arthur L. Kobler, a Seattle psychologist, plowed through the subject of misusing the computer. The use of the computer, they concede, inevitably will increase. But it is being called on to act in areas where man cannot define his own ability. There is a tendency to let the machine treat special problems as if they were routine calculations; for example, it may be used to plot the route for a new highway by a routine computation of physical factors. But the computation may overlook the importance of locating the highway where it will not create or compound ugliness.

Johnson and Kobler also feel that the "current tendency of men to give up individual identity and escape from responsibility" is enhanced by the computer. It takes man's inputs and turns out a neat, clean, consistent judgment without "obsessive hesitation," commitments, or emotional involvements. In effect, it assumes responsibility; and its neatness and decisiveness can lead men to skip value judgments, to accept unimaginative and partial results as accurate solutions, and to read into its results the ability to solve all problems. Even scientists who are aware of the limitations of machines, the authors reason, can find them so useful in solving narrow and well-defined problems that they may tend to assume the computer can solve all problems. Thus the danger of oversimplifying complex decisions, a danger that has always existed, becomes worse. Another worry is that military computer systems will react so swiftly that the people who nominally make the judgments will not have time to make them. "The need for caution," Johnson and Kobler conclude, "will be greater in the future. Until we can determine more perfectly what we want from the machines, let us not call on mechanized decision systems to act upon human systems without realistic human processing. As we proceed with the inevitable development of computers and artificial intelligence, let us be sure we know what we are doing."

Military and computer experts are already studying the problems raised by the speed of the machines. And to use the warnings to deny the real value of computers would be as foolish as misusing computers. The machines compel men to formulate their problems so much more intelligently and more thoroughly than they ever have that men can hardly be unaware of the shortcomings of their programs. The great majority of computers, as Johnson and Kobler are well aware, are being employed by business. Granted that U.S. business makes mistakes, granted that it has made and will make mistakes with computers, it does not operate in a monopolistic vacuum. Nothing would make a company more vulnerable to smart competitors than to abdicate responsibility to the neat, clean, consistent judgments of a machine.

The computer is here to stay; it cannot be shelved any more than the telescope or the steam engine could have been shelved. Taking everything together, man has a stupendous thing working for him, and one is not being egregiously optimistic to suggest he will make the most of it. Precisely because man is so arduously trying to imitate the behavior of human beings in the computer, he is bound to improve enormously his understanding of both himself and the machine.

Index